stranger in
the mirror

This book is dedicated to Hazel, my darling wife.
Without your dedication, love and support, this book would
not have been possible.

To my beautiful daughters, Beckie and Heather.
Thank you for your friendship and your love.

To Keith and Myra Ashworth,
and Jim and Lilian Bradshaw,
my parents in the faith.

To all our Partners in the ministry
who have made this book possible.

stranger in the mirror

Don Egan

ISBN 0 9525240 8 2

Scripture quotations, unless otherwise indicated, are from the
New King James Version.

Cover design by Peter Goodsell

Published by **The Evangelism Fellowship,**
P O Box 55, STOWMARKET, Suffolk, IP14 1UG, England.

Contents

Acknowledgements

I would like to thank Linda Ottewell for all her help in proof-reading and suggesting changes to the text.

My thanks also to Ray Gilbert for negotiating with printers and helping greatly with the production side of things.

Also, thanks to Peter Goodsell for the excellent cover design.

I am grateful to Andy Economides who encouraged me to press on writing this book after many false starts. Thanks also to J John for investing time and resources into this ministry - it has made the difference between giving up and pressing on to fulfil God's calling on my life.

1. Stranger in the Mirror

Many people today feel overwhelmed by life. Even those who seem to have 'got it together' sometimes feel bewildered by the ever increasing demands made upon them. A survey once showed that on an average day, the average person feels a little less than average. Something deep within human beings tells them that there is more to life than money, sex, work and friends. As good as all those things are, in the right place, for many of us, life still aches.

Sometimes we have that disturbing experience of looking into the mirror and seeing a stranger staring back at us. We look into the eyes of our reflection and somehow don't recognise ourselves. We stare deep into our own soul, but see a blank space. This insecurity about our identity, and about life, affects everything we do. All across the world, the cry of the human heart is, 'Who am I?'

Albert Einstein said, *"Reality is merely an illusion, albeit a very persistent one."*

Sometimes, with hindsight, we manage to make sense of part of our life. Yet the overall picture still confuses us. Life is best understood backwards, but has to be lived forwards. Our surroundings and the rapid pace of life add to the feeling of uncertainty. We live at such a speed, that the world can be a confusing place. The unrelenting advance of technological development shows no sign of slowing down.

Al Gore, Vice President of the USA, said, *"We have constructed in our civilisation a false world of plastic flowers and astroturf, air conditioning and fluorescent lights, windows that don't open and background music that never stops, days when we don't know whether it has rained, nights when the sky never stops glowing, Walkman and Watchman cocoons, frozen food for the microwave oven, sleepy hearts jump-started by caffeine, alcohol, drugs and illusions."* He was talking about the environment but he could have just as easily been talking about this cry of the human soul.

When I was growing up, men landed on the moon and computers sprang up in every area of life. It felt as if the brave new world was emerging before my eyes. Man had become the god of his own destiny.

I used to read comics, as a teenager, about a futuristic world where robots did all the housework, everyone was at leisure and poverty and sickness had been eradicated. Yet this Utopia has never materialised. We seem to have more crime, more poverty and more sickness than ever before.

Charles Handy, the business guru, wrote, *"Sometimes it seems that the more we know, the more confused we get; that the more we increase our technical capacity the more powerless we become. With all our sophisticated armaments we can only watch impotently as parts of the world kill each other. We grow more food than we need but cannot feed the starving. We can unravel the mysteries of galaxies but not of our own families."*

We busy ourselves with many things and yet the key questions remain unanswered. Everything has been figured out, except how to live. The world seems to be rushing headlong towards an uncertain destination. Much of life has become computerised, but young people, those most at ease with the world of computers, wear T-shirts emblazoned with the slogan *"Rage against the machine."* Apparently the human spirit does not run under Windows.

For decades in Britain, the individual was exalted as the answer to all our economic problems. We were even told that there was no such thing as society. Yet the loneliness that permeates so much of society exposes the truth that we need someone other than ourselves. Charles Handy wrote, *"It is a paradox, one best captured by Jung, who said, years ago, that we need others to be truly ourselves. 'I' needs 'We' to be fully 'I'. Looking up, however, at the office blocks in every city, those little boxes piled on top of each other up into the sky, one has to wonder how much room there is for 'I' amid the filing cabinets and the terminals."*

I suspect housewives, too, often wonder how much room there is for 'I' amid the washing machines, cookers and school-runs of everyday life. It sometimes seems that the whole of society has lost its identity, its basis for existence. In his book *'Beyond Certainty'*, Charles Handy writes,

"Many would like to go 'Back to Basics', as Britain's John Major sensed when he made it his rallying call..., but it turned out that no one knew what the basics were. There is no certainty any more. We aren't even sure what life itself is for; if, indeed, it is anything more than a genetic accident."

As we look at the stranger in the mirror, we sometimes dare to wonder if there is a God who cares about us. St Paul wrote to the church at Corinth, *"Now we see in a mirror, dimly, but then face to face. Now I know in part, but then I shall know just as I also am known."* (1 Corinthians 13:12).

There are some things which we will never fully understand before we meet God face to face. Yet we can know God here in this life. We can get to know God through what he has said in his word, the Bible. Jesus himself, is called "the Word." Through him we can get to know the living God personally. James, the brother of Jesus, wrote, *"If anyone is a hearer of the word and not a doer, he is like a man observing his natural face in a mirror; for he observes himself, goes away, and immediately forgets what kind of man he was. But he who looks into the perfect law of liberty and continues in it, and is not a forgetful hearer but a doer of the work, this one will be blessed in what he does."* (James 1:23-25).

A friend of mine tells a moving story of meeting his father for the first time. My friend had been adopted at birth and all his life he struggled with his own identity. When, late in life, he finally met his father, he found they had little in common. Yet something was satisfied deep within him. Nothing could make up for all those years of searching, but at last, he had come home.

We, too, have been estranged from our Creator and it has induced in us a searching for something. We also have amnesia - we're not really sure what it is we are looking for. There was something that was ours that would make us complete, but we have lost it. And we will never find rest until we discover it. It *can* be found now, in this life, and when we find it, it will be a real homecoming.

When we look into the mirror and wonder who we really are, we are suffering from a loss of identity. We have forgotten that we are made in God's image. To recover our identity we must first discover God. Just as the Queen's head validates our bank notes, so the image of God in us validates human life. When God appeared to Moses in the burning bush to call him to lead the people out of Egypt, there were two key issues. In Exodus 3:11 Moses says, *"Who am I that I should go to Pharaoh, and that I should bring the children of Israel out of Egypt?"* In verse 13 he asks God who he is. Effectively he is saying, *'Who am I and who are you?'* Understanding who we are and who God is, will release us to reach our full potential. In Matthew 16, Jesus asks the disciples the same questions. *"When Jesus came into the region of Caesarea Philippi, He asked His disciples, saying, "Who do men say that I, the Son of Man, am?" So they said, "Some say John the Baptist, some Elijah, and others Jeremiah or one of the prophets." He said to them, "But who do you say that I am?" Simon Peter answered and said, "You are the Christ, the Son of the living God."* (Matthew

16:13-16). This understanding of who Jesus is, is fundamental to understanding who we are.

Jesus is the central figure of history. We will look at this more in the next chapter, but for now it is sufficient to say that more books have been written about Jesus than any other person in history. An unknown writer wrote these words about the life of Jesus Christ.

"He was born in an obscure village, the child of a peasant woman. He grew up in another obscure village where he worked in a carpenter's shop until he was thirty. He never wrote a book. He never held office. He never had a family or owned a house. He never went to college. He never visited a big city. He never travelled more than 200 miles from where he was born. He did none of those things usually associated with greatness. He had no credentials but himself.

He was only thirty three when the tide of public opinion turned against him. His friends ran away. One of them denied him. He was turned over to his enemies and went through the mockery of a trial. He was nailed to a cross between two thieves. While dying, his executioners gambled for his clothing. When he was dead he was laid in a borrowed grave through the pity of a friend.

Nineteen centuries have come and gone, and today he is the central figure of the human race and the leader of mankind's progress. All the armies that have ever marched, all the navies that have ever sailed, all the parliaments that have ever sat, all the kings that have ever reigned, put together, have not affected the life on earth of mankind as powerfully as that one solitary life."

If ever the glory of God was reflected in the life of a human being, it was seen in the life of Jesus. The way to find our identity, the way to find a new life of freedom, the way to enter through the veil of the dimly lit mirror, is to know him and become like him. St Paul wrote, *"And we, who with unveiled faces all reflect the Lord's glory, are being transformed into his likeness with ever-increasing glory, which comes from the Lord, who is the Spirit."* (2 Corinthians 3:18).

The way for us to come home is through the one who said, *"I am the Way... no one comes to the Father but by me."* (John 14:6). Like my friend who was adopted, we can come home. Through Jesus we can come to the end of our search. We can finish being a stranger to ourselves and to God. St Paul said, *"Therefore remember... that at that time you were without Christ, being aliens from the commonwealth of Israel and strangers from the covenants of promise, having no hope and without God in the world. But now in Christ Jesus you who once were far off have been brought near by the blood of Christ."* (Ephesians 2:11-13).

Jesus used many pictures to describe this estrangement of the human race from their Creator. He spoke about the lost sheep, the lost coin and the lost son. He said his mission was to seek and to save that which was lost. His purpose was to restore us to this relationship with the Father.

A human being looking for God is like a mouse looking for a cat. While you are searching for him, God is searching for you. He is looking for a way to attract your attention so you can come home and reach your full potential.

In the story of the lost son, the son decides to return to his father, not as a son, but as a servant. The father's response is not what we would expect. He doesn't ask 'where have you been?' or 'what have you done?' If you are trapped in a mess right now, Jesus' story gives you great hope. See how the Father is waiting to receive you.

"After he had spent everything, there was a severe famine in that whole country, and he began to be in need. So he went and

hired himself out to a citizen of that country, who sent him to his fields to feed pigs. He longed to fill his stomach with the pods that the pigs were eating, but no-one gave him anything. When he came to his senses, he said, `How many of my father's hired men have food to spare, and here I am starving to death! I will set out and go back to my father and say to him: Father, I have sinned against heaven and against you.

I am no longer worthy to be called your son; make me like one of your hired men.'

So he got up and went to his father. "But while he was still a long way off, his father saw him and was filled with compassion for him; he ran to his son, threw his arms around him and kissed him.

The son said to him, `Father, I have sinned against heaven and against you. I am no longer worthy to be called your son.'

"But the father said to his servants, `Quick! Bring the best robe and put it on him. Put a ring on his finger and sandals on his feet. Bring the fattened calf and kill it. Let's have a feast and celebrate. For this son of mine was dead and is alive again; he was lost and is found.' So they began to celebrate." (Luke 15:14-24).

God is calling you to come home today. He wants you to know that there is a Father who loves you, who blesses you, who likes you and wants the best for you. Come home today and rest from your long journey. The Bible is the map and compass for your journey. *"Your word is a lamp to my feet and a light to my path."* (Psalm 119:105). I believe that as you give attention to what God says about you in the Bible, you will discover who you are, who he is, and your relationship with him. The first thing he says to you is:

"My son, pay attention to what I say; listen closely to my words. Do not let them out of your sight, keep them within your

13

heart; for they are life to those who find them and health to a man's whole body.

Above all else, guard your heart, for it is the wellspring of life. Put away perversity from your mouth; keep corrupt talk far from your lips. Let your eyes look straight ahead, fix your gaze directly before you. Make level paths for your feet and take only ways that are firm. Do not swerve to the right or the left; keep your foot from evil." (Proverbs 4:20-27).

Every book has a first chapter. I pray that this may be the first chapter of your restoration and finding your true destiny, and the discovery of who you really are in God.

2. Cross Purposes

Lots of people died on a cross. It was the Roman way of making a gruesome example out of offenders. So what is so special about Jesus? If Jesus was just like any other person, why does it matter that he, like many others at the time, died a horrible death on a cross?

If we think of Jesus as being like any other person, we will always be thinking and talking at cross purposes, rather than understanding the purpose of the cross.

Lots of people have opinions about Jesus. Some of the more popular opinions don't really stand up to scrutiny. They've not really been thought through properly. Take the three most common ones for example.

Jesus was just a great moral teacher.

Jesus was just a prophet.

Jesus was just one of many religious leaders.

Certainly Jesus was and is all of these things. But when people say that he was *'just...'* these things, they become hard to reconcile with the facts.

Just a great moral teacher?

No one's teaching has affected the moral life of the world as much as Jesus' has. But the snag with him being just a great moral teacher is that he claimed to be God in human form. So what does it say for his morals if he was trying to deceive crowds of people into thinking he was God? If he himself was deluded, what does it say for his sanity if he believed he was God when he wasn't? Could such great world-changing teaching come from a lunatic?

People who claim to be God fall into one of three categories. They are liars, lunatics or telling the truth (if they are God). There have been many liars who claimed to be God, just as

Jesus said there would be, *"Watch out that no one deceives you. For many will come in my name, claiming, 'I am the Christ, ' and will deceive many."* But the life of the deceiver never matches up to their claims, and sooner or later the deception becomes obvious.

Lunatics are characterised by a confused life and confused thoughts. They are out of touch with reality. One of the reasons Jesus had such an impact was that his life matched his words and his teaching. There was order and peace about everything he said and did. There was never any scandal attached to him. His whole personality was transparently good.

Nobody at the time thought he was just a good moral teacher. They understood his claims to be God perfectly. They either loved him or hated him. No one was indifferent towards him. *'Again the Jews picked up stones to stone him, but Jesus said to them, "I have shown you many great miracles from the Father. For which of these do you stone me?"*

" We are not stoning you for any of these," replied the Jews, " but for blasphemy, because you, a mere man, claim to be God." (John 10:33).

In fact, there was one person who tried to call Jesus just a good teacher, but Jesus' reaction to that is interesting. *"As Jesus started on his way, a man ran up to him and fell on his knees before him. "Good teacher," he asked, "what must I do to inherit eternal life?"*

" Why do you call me good?" Jesus answered. "No one is good, except God alone."

Jesus wasn't having such a statement left unchallenged. He cannot be pinned down to being just a good teacher. Because of his lifestyle, it is also hard to believe he was either a madman or a deceiver.

Just a prophet?

Certainly Jesus was a prophet. He prophesied many things which have come to pass. But Jesus was more a fulfilment of prophecy. The Old Testament is full of prophecies about the coming Messiah.

It said he would be born of the tribe of Judah in Genesis 49.
It said he would be born in Bethlehem in Micah 5.
It said he would be born of a virgin in Isaiah 7.
It said he would be called out of Egypt in Hosea 11.
It said he would be a prophet in Deuteronomy 18.
It said his own people would reject him in Isaiah 53.
It said he would be betrayed and sold for 30 pieces of silver in Zechariah 11.
It said he would be put to death by crucifixion in Psalm 22.
It said soldiers would cast lots for his clothing in Psalm 22.
It said he would be raised from the dead in Psalm 16.
It said he would ascend to heaven in Psalm 68.

In fact, there are 322 prophecies about the Messiah in the Old Testament. The chances of all those prophecies coming true in the life of one person are incredibly small.

The more we prophesy about a particular person or event, the greater the odds against it happening. For example, if I prophesy that it will snow on Christmas Day, I have a 1 in 2 chance of being right. If I prophesy that it will snow and Bing Crosby will be on TV singing *'I'm dreaming of a white Christmas'*, the odds now double to 1 in 4.

By the law of compound mathematics, the odds of 322 things prophesied coming true, in the life of one person, are a staggering 1 in 8,400,00010. *(That's one in eight million, four hundred thousand to the power of ten)*. So to say Jesus was just a prophet, is a bit of an understatement.

Just a religious leader?

It is true there have been many great leaders who have spoken about God and who had powerful lives. There have been many who have brought to the world formidable philosophies that have affected the course of history. Names like Buddha, Gandhi, Mohammed and Karl Marx immediately spring to mind.

But there is a significant difference between Jesus and any other leader that we could name. We can visit the graves of past leaders because they are dead. But the grave of Jesus is empty.

Jesus stands out from all other leaders in history. The whole premise of Christianity is that Jesus is alive from the dead and we can know him personally today. So to say Jesus was just a great moral teacher, just a prophet, or just one of many religious leaders doesn't stand up to the evidence. In fact, being so patronising about him just shows our ignorance. Jesus cannot be damned with faint praise.

Sometimes people say, '*Jesus never claimed to be the Son of God*'. It sounds intelligent but, again, it doesn't really fit the real evidence. So let's look at what he did say.

In the gospel accounts Jesus constantly claims to be God. That's why the religious rulers kept trying to stone him to death for blasphemy. Let's take just four statements Jesus made:

"I am God's Son" (John 10:36). *"No one comes to the Father except through me."* (John 14:6). *"Anyone who has seen me has seen the Father." (John* 14:9). *"He who believes in me will live, even though he dies."* (John 11:25)

If Jesus was lying when he said these things then the gospels contain the worst blasphemy known to man. Many religious leaders have said that they have had special insights into God, but Jesus stands alone in history as one claiming to be God and yet being taken seriously by reasonable thinking people.

Just imagine, for a moment, anyone you know making these claims. Even the person you respect most would seem preposterous if he or she said these things. The only explanation that really fits the facts is that Jesus was who he said he was - God in human form. But there is another reason why we need to understand who Jesus is.

Our personal need.

Even the most accomplished human beings today speak of an *'aching emptiness deep inside'* them. People, even the most affluent people, speak of something missing from life. Nothing seems to satisfy deep down.

Bob Geldof, speaking to Q magazine, said, *"One night I ate hashish and tried to kill myself. I fell asleep with the radio tuned to white noise pressed against my ear. It was horrific. That thing I tapped into inside me was so untouchably dark."*

Albert Einstein in a letter to a friend, wrote, *"It is strange to be known so universally and yet be so lonely."*

And all that society seems to offer us is an advertiser's dream. The spirit of the age calls to us from every television screen, *'Buy your way out of misery'*. We are offered a new designer life, where the implication is, *'Buy our product and you can be as happy as these people are.'* These people who live in a world that is spotlessly clean, without poverty, and where the worst thing that could happen is that your soap powder doesn't quite get your whites really white. The adverts get our attention because they are asking us the question we are asking ourselves, *'Who am I? Who is the stranger I see in the mirror?'*

Bernard Levin wrote some years ago, *"Countries like ours are full of people who have all the material comforts they desire, together with such non-material blessings as a happy family, and yet lead lives of quiet, and at times, noisy, desperation. Understanding nothing but the fact that there is a hole inside them and that however much food and drink they pour into it, however many motor cars and television sets they stuff it with, however many well-balanced children and loyal friends they parade around the edges of it... it aches."*

Why do we need Jesus?

Jesus' prime purpose in coming to earth was to meet this deepest need we have, this cry of the human heart. Jesus said *"I have come that they might have life and have it to the full"*

The Bible teaches that we were cut off from knowing God by this darkness inside us. The emptiness we feel can only be satisfied by God because the place that is empty in our heart was designed only for him. The hole inside us is God-shaped. Nothing else will fit. All the things we try to fill it with are like the wrong part of the jigsaw. It's only when we ask Jesus to come and fill that emptiness that we find the missing peace.

Anyway, why would you want to refuse Jesus his rightful place in your life? Consider who he is for a moment. This Jesus who came to the world in humility. This Jesus who opened the eyes of the blind; who unstopped the ears of the deaf; who made the lame to walk and the dumb to speak.

Consider this Jesus who commanded the winds and the waves to be still and they obeyed him.

This Jesus who stopped a funeral procession in the village of Nain. Opening the coffin he brought a little boy back to life and gave him to his widowed mother.

This Jesus, who came weeping into Bethany Cemetery and cried out to a man four days dead, "Lazarus! Come out!" And there before the amazed crowd the dead man walked out.

Consider this Jesus, falsely arrested, put through the mockery of a trial. Blindfolded, punched, kicked and spat upon, and whipped till he was almost dead.

Consider this Jesus, whose healing hands were nailed to a cross - each agonising blow of the hammer causing torture to the hands that healed.

Consider this Jesus, whose feet had walked in obedience to his Father for 33 years, now being nailed down.

Consider that beautiful face, with the eyes from which such perfect love shone out; that face now defaced as a crown of thorns was pressed into it.

A scientist was examining the process of death during crucifixion. He discovered *'that if the whole weight of the body had been taken on the crucified, spread-eagled arms, the victim would have died very swiftly from suffocation. It was for that reason that the feet were also nailed to the cross. They took some of the weight, preventing that pulling down and constriction of the rib-cage which would have brought an earlier release.*

There was thus a constant shifting in the position of the crucified: he would slump down, his weight on the nails in his wrist. Soon the pressure across his chest and the restriction of his breathing would force him forward and up, putting his weight now on the nail through his feet. After a while the agony this caused would force him to drop again. So it would go, hour after hour, the slow agonised rise, the appalling collapse...'

And there, as Jesus bled and suffocated to death, his heart was filled with love for you. This was no mere martyrdom. Jesus said he was purposely laying down his life for you. *"I lay down my life - only to take it up again. No one takes it from me, but I lay it down of my own accord. I have authority to lay it down and authority to take it up again."*

The Bible says that Jesus is the only way to God. In order to find real life that will satisfy, we must receive Jesus into our hearts and into our lives. The Bible calls this process 'salvation': *"Salvation is found in no one else, for there is no other name under heaven given to men by which we must be saved."*

The Bible clearly teaches that those who reject Jesus in this life will be rejected by God in the life to come. The Bible says,

"He who has the Son has life; he who does not have the Son of God does not have life."

Jesus said, *"If anyone is ashamed of me and my words, the Son of Man will be ashamed of him when he comes in his glory and in the glory of the Father"*

Our need for Jesus is not primarily about our happiness but about our forgiveness. We could say that we don't need God to make us happy. But only the most arrogant and proud person could say that they don't need forgiveness.

Jesus didn't come to condemn us but to save us from this separation from God. The reason we need Jesus in our lives is so we can begin to have a relationship with God.

In fact, Christianity is not something we try to do. It is someone we receive. We could never live a life like Jesus did or taught on our own. That's why we need to receive Jesus personally into our hearts and into our lives.

William Temple said, *"It is no good giving me a play like Hamlet or King Lear, and telling me to write a play like that. Shakespeare could do it; I can't. And it is no good showing me a life like the life of Jesus and telling me to live a life like that. Jesus could do it; I can't. But if the genius of Shakespeare could come and live in me, then I could write plays like that. And if the Spirit of Jesus could come and live in me, I could live a life like that."*

What does he want from me?

In the Bible, Jesus says he wants to come into your heart, into your life, so that you can have a relationship with him. Jesus calls you first of all to himself - not to a particular church, not to a set of rules or some philosophy or religion. He calls you to himself.

He stands at the doorway to your life, and his words are like knocks on the door to get your attention. What he wants from you is that you would open yourself to him, so that he can meet with you and give you real life.

He says to you, *"Here I am! I stand at the door and knock. If anyone hears my voice and opens the door, I will come in and eat with him, and he with me."* (Revelation 3:20).

How can you open the door? To open yourself to Jesus you have to invite him to come in. He wants to meet with you honestly and openly. He knows everything you have ever done and because of his death on the cross, he accepts you unconditionally.

So picture him standing before you now. And speak out these words to him. Say them out loud as you offer yourself to him.

Dear Jesus.
I want to know you today.
Please forgive me for the past.
For all the things I wish I hadn't done.
For all the good things I wish I had done but didn't.
(Take a moment to mention specific things...)
I believe you gave your life on the cross for me.
I now give my life to you.
Come into my life today.
Come in as my Saviour to give me life.
Come in as my Lord to guide me.
Come in as my Friend to be with me.
Fill me with your Holy Spirit and give me a new life.
And I will serve you for the rest of my life.
Amen.

If you have said this prayer and meant it, Jesus has come into your life. In order to maintain this new life there are a few things you need to do. You have entered into a new relationship with Jesus. Any relationship that is starved of conversation will grow cold and die. So you need to **talk with Jesus every day.**

The best way to do this is to **read some of his words in the Bible** (preferably in a modern translation - The Good News or The New International Version are good ones). You'll find the words of Jesus about two-thirds of the way through the Bible in the books of Matthew, Mark, Luke and John. (Use the contents page if you can't find them!)

After reading some of his words, talk to him and ask him to be involved in your day. Many people find first thing in the morning a good time for this, so they take God into the day with them.

In coming into this new relationship with Jesus, you have also come into a new relationship with God's family. So **find a church** where you can grow in your new relationship and where you can learn more of Jesus and make new friends. Church should be a friendly, encouraging and exciting place to be.

Many churches today have housegroups or homegroups - a few people meet together during the week in someone's home to look at the Bible and learn together. Speak to the leader of the church about joining one of these.

It's also important not to be shy about what you have done. Tell someone what you have done today. Start with someone you think will be pleased to hear. Never apologise for being a Christian.

When I prayed a prayer like this in 1976 I never imagined it would be so important as I now realise. It was, without doubt, the most important step I have ever taken in my life. If you prayed this prayer, write to me at the address on the back of this book. I'd love to hear from you.

3. That's the Spirit!

When Jesus returned to his Father in heaven, he said he would send another Comforter, the Holy Spirit. From the day of Pentecost recorded in Acts 2, it has been possible to have the same Spirit that lived in Jesus, living in a believer. The Holy Spirit is literally the Spirit of God (John 4:24). The personal unseen force who intervenes in the affairs of human beings. The Holy Spirit is the one who brings about the new birth of the Christian (John 3:5), the one who heals, delivers from evil, and brings to us the peace that passes understanding. Jesus told his disciples to wait for the empowering of the Holy Spirit before they began to witness for him (Luke 24:49). John the Baptist told his followers that Jesus would baptise people with the Holy Spirit (Luke 3:16).

Such is the Spirit's power that Christians sometimes refer to the Spirit as 'it' instead of 'he'. But the Holy Spirit is not an 'it', a vague source of spiritual power. The Holy Spirit is 'he', the personal third person of the Trinity, who breathes the divine life into our bodies (Genesis 2:7).

The Church of today cries out for spiritual life. It seems unbelievable that the Church, whose founding fathers were martyred because of controversy, is thought by many people to be dull and boring. Visiting some churches, you might be forgiven for thinking that Jesus said to Nicodemus, *'You must be bored again'!*

A young couple moved to a new area and tried to become members of the local Church. Unfortunately, they were made quite unwelcome. They went to see the vicar and told him that no one spoke to them, the children were hushed, and no one helped them follow the service. The vicar told them to pray to God about it. A few weeks later they met the vicar in town and he asked if God had answered their prayers. They said God had told them not to worry, because he'd been trying to get into that Church for years but now he goes somewhere else!

For many reasons, down through history, Christians have kept the Holy Spirit out of the Church. There have been decades, and sometimes centuries, in history, when the flame of the Spirit has been reduced to a tiny unseen pilot light. This is why any movement of the Spirit seems unusual to many people today. But in God's eyes, any movement of the Holy Spirit is normal. It is mediocrity that is foreign to him!

Before we look at the more sensational activities of the Holy Spirit, we would do well to understand more of who he is.

The Spirit of Creation

The Bible says the Holy Spirit was there at creation. *"In the beginning God created the heavens and the earth... and the Spirit of God was hovering over the waters."* (Genesis 1:2). This is one of the hallmarks of the Holy Spirit. He builds up, encourages, creates new things. It is the Holy Spirit who gives us a new heart and causes us to want to please God (Ezekiel 36:26).

Thousands of Christians throughout history have been moved by the Holy Spirit to begin a new work, make a new discovery, or change the course of history.

Sir Isaac Newton is best remembered for his law of gravity and work on the physics of light. Yet he believed that his scientific discoveries were communicated to him by the Holy Spirit, and he regarded the understanding of scripture as more important than his scientific work.

Hudson Taylor stood on Brighton beach in the 1800's, and felt such a movement of the Holy Spirit in his heart, drawing him to move to China and establish the China Inland Mission.

George Fox climbed Pendle Hill in the North of England and had such an encounter with the Holy Spirit that he later founded the Quaker movement as an antidote to dead religion.

Before Jesus walked the earth the Holy Spirit had only been seen in small measure.

The Spirit in the Old Testament

In the Old Testament, the Holy Spirit was only given to certain individuals, in certain situations, in only one nation - Israel. People like Abraham, Moses, Elijah, Elisha, King David, Isaiah, and Ezekiel, all had the Holy Spirit evident in their lives. This limitation was not God's ideal, but a result of the fall of mankind in the garden of Eden. Although these people did some staggering miracles through the power of the Holy Spirit, God's desire was that all his children might know that close relationship with him. A relationship which would be punctuated with the grace and power of the Holy Spirit .

Towards the end of the Old Testament period, God's desire is declared by the prophet Joel, *"I will pour out my Spirit on all people. Your sons and daughters will prophesy, your old men will dream dreams, your young men will see visions. Even on my servants, both men and women, I will pour out my Spirit in those days."* (Joel 2:28-29). The glorious beauty of this promise is that no one need be left out. The Holy Spirit is not just for priest or prophet. He's for young and old. He's for men and women, sons and daughters, even lowly servants!

The Spirit in Jesus

The Holy Spirit was perhaps best demonstrated in the life of Jesus. He became human when he was conceived by the Holy Spirit in the womb of Mary (Luke 1:35). The Holy Spirit descended on Jesus with a special anointing at the start of his public ministry (Luke 3:22). Jesus was filled with the Holy Spirit from birth, but this was the Father's first public authentication of the Son of God, and the sign recognised by John the Baptist (John 1:33-34). The Holy Spirit drove Jesus into the wilderness for 40 days (Luke 4:1-2). He returned from the wilderness in the power of the Holy Spirit, to Galilee. He went up to the temple and read from Isaiah, *"The Spirit of the Sovereign Lord is on me, because the Lord has anointed me to preach good news to the poor..."* (Isaiah 61:1).

The burning question of the day was, Who is Jesus? Jesus asked them, *"Who do the crowds say I am?"* They replied, *"Some say John the Baptist; others say Elijah; and still others, that one of the prophets of long ago has come back to life."* (Luke 9:19). He was suspected of being an Old Testament prophet - in other words, a person who displayed the power and grace of the Holy Spirit in his life. However, Jesus taught the disciples that his power and character were what God wanted in the life of every Christian. He said, *"I tell you the truth, anyone who has faith in me will do what I have been doing. He will do even greater things than these, because I am going to the Father."* (John 14:12).

"...because I am going to the Father..." Jesus indicates here and elsewhere (John 7:39), that the promised Holy Spirit would be given as a result of his death and resurrection. The baptism of the Holy Spirit is only possible through the cross. And the Holy Spirit was not absent from Jesus' suffering on the cross.

In Hebrews 9:14 we read of *"...Christ, who through the eternal Spirit offered himself unblemished to God..."* Just as the Holy Spirit was at work in the conception of Christ, so he was at work when Jesus gave up his life on the cross to save us from sin. To know the baptism of the Holy Spirit we must first know Jesus. He not only paid the price for this gift, but he is the One who baptises with the Holy Spirit (Luke 3:16).

The Spirit at Pentecost.

Pentecost was the Jewish festival of first-fruits. It was 50 days after the Passover, the time of Jesus' crucifixion. The festival was significant: as the Holy Spirit was poured out on the disciples (Acts 2), the crowd encountered the first-fruits of ordinary men filled with the life and power of Jesus. The Spirit came suddenly and supernaturally. Tongues of fire appeared on the disciples. They spoke in foreign languages they hadn't learnt. Their audience, from many different countries, would have found it hard following their difficult Galilean speech. Yet everyone heard the wonders of God in their own language. The curse of Babel (Genesis 11) was dramatically reversed. From this moment the disciples were transformed. The dynamic Christian Church was born. Just as Jesus promised, they began to do not only the things he had done, but even greater things. The Acts of the Apostles charts the development of this explosion of God's power in the life of Christian believers.

Did the Holy Spirit's power cease with the first apostles?

Some Christians teach that the supernatural aspects of the Holy Spirit died out with the first apostles. They believe the Apostolic period was a special dispensation. However, this teaching has no basis in scripture. It may have developed as a reason for the absence of any dynamic activity in the life of some churches. But we must not base belief solely on our experience. It must be rooted in the plain reading of scripture. And such a fundamental belief would need to be based on the whole view of scripture, not just an odd text or two plucked out of context. A text without a context can easily become a pretext.

Dispensationalists, as such Christians are known, sometimes quote St Paul when he wrote to the Corinthians, *"Where there are prophecies, they will cease; where there are tongues, they will be stilled; where there is knowledge, it will pass away. For we know in part and we prophesy in part, but when perfection comes, the imperfect disappears."* (1 Corinthians 13:8-10). But that is to take the scripture out of context, because Paul goes on... *"Now we see but a poor reflection as in a mirror; then we shall see face to face. Now I know in part; then I shall know fully, even as I am fully known."* (1 Corinthians 13:12). This verse makes it clear that Paul is not talking about the end of some apostolic period. He is talking about when we get to heaven and meet Jesus face to face. The supernatural activity of the Holy Spirit did not die out with the apostles. Church history is a catalogue of the Holy Spirit's activity.

The Spirit in History

The Holy Spirit has long been recognised as the One who brings faith alive, who reveals the reality of Jesus, who transforms belief from a dull assent to certain doctrines, to a life-changing faith.

Thomas à Kempis (1380-1471) wrote, *"Many people, although they often hear the Gospel, feel little desire to follow it, because they lack the Spirit of Christ"*

Jesus said of the Spirit, *"The wind blows wherever it pleases. You hear its sound, but you cannot tell where it comes from or where it is going. So it is with everyone born of the Spirit."* (John 3:8). Like the wind, the Holy Spirit is sometimes a gentle breeze, sometimes a violent wind (Acts 2:2). The power of God that is visiting the churches in our day is often accompanied by deep emotional experiences which have become controversial. Yet the strange experiences of certain people in our day, which are attributed to the Holy Spirit, are not new. The deep emotions and falling under the Spirit are evident in history.

In the 1700's, revivalist preachers, John Wesley and George Whitefield, observed strange manifestations when they preached the gospel. One account commented, *"That the audience should groan, and scream, and faint, and sink to the ground convulsively is so unusual that many are at a loss to explain this phenomenon."* Apparently, when George Whitefield himself first heard of these manifestations at John Wesley's meetings, he objected to such demonstrations. Concerning this, Wesley wrote in his journal, *"I had opportunity to talk to Mr Whitefield of those outward signs which so often accompanied the inward work of God. I found his objections were chiefly grounded on gross misrepresentations... But the next day, he had an opportunity of informing himself better; for no sooner had he begun, in the application of his sermon, to invite all sinners to believe in Christ, than four persons sunk down close to him, almost in the same moment... From this time, I trust, we shall all suffer God to carry on His own work in the way that pleaseth Him."*

It was the revival which began in Azusa Street, Los Angeles, in 1906, which brought the biblical practice of baptism in the Holy Spirit, back into focus in Britain. This three-year-long meeting was attended by leaders from North America, Europe and the Third World. It was the beginning of the current Pentecostal movement in Britain.

In the 1960's, the spread of the charismatic movement into the main denominations broke down many barriers to the work of the Holy Spirit.

From the day of Pentecost until now, the Holy Spirit has been at work to convict people of their need for Christ. When we ask Jesus to come and be our personal Saviour, our past sin is forgiven. However, God offers a new power for living which adds a supernatural dimension to faith in Christ. This is expressed in the scriptures as the Fruit of the Spirit and the Gifts of the Spirit.

The Fruit of the Spirit

The Fruit of the Spirit gives us the character of Jesus. Like fruit, it takes time to grow. When we ask God to baptise us with the Holy Spirit, this fruit begins to grow in our life. The fruit of the Spirit is listed in Galatians 5:22-23.

"The fruit of the Spirit is love, joy, peace, patience, kindness, goodness, faithfulness, gentleness and self-control."

This list describes the character of Jesus. The Holy Spirit wants to grow this fruit in the life of the Christian.

The Gifts of the Spirit

The Gifts of the Holy Spirit give us the power of Jesus. He said that those who believe in him will do the things he did (John 14:12). The gifts of the Spirit describe the power of Jesus. The gifts are not like the fruits in that they don't grow, they are given. We may learn more of how they work as we go along, but they come ready to use on the first day we receive them. The gifts are listed in 1 Corinthians 12:7-11, *"Now to each one the manifestation of the Spirit is given for the common good. To one there is given through the Spirit the message of wisdom, to another the message of knowledge by means of the same Spirit, to another faith by the same Spirit, to another gifts of healing by that one Spirit, to another miraculous powers, to another prophecy, to another distinguishing between spirits, to another speaking in different kinds of tongues, and to still another the interpretation of tongues. All these are the work of one and the same Spirit, and he gives them to each one, just as he determines."*

All these gifts, apart from tongues and interpretation, were seen in the Old Testament at certain times. What are all these gifts for?

Firstly, Paul indicates that they are not to build up an individual into a super hero, *"... the manifestation of the Spirit is given for the common good."* So in a congregation the Holy Spirit will distribute these gifts to build up his body, the Church.

Secondly, it may help to explain very briefly what each one is:

Gift of Wisdom and the Gift of Knowledge

These two gifts go together. This has nothing to do with natural wisdom or knowledge, but something which the Holy Spirit reveals to a person which they could not otherwise have known.

If you are given the gift of knowledge you really need to pray for the gift of wisdom - *'what shall I do with this knowledge?'* Or make a close friendship with someone who has been given the gift of wisdom. When we are given knowledge by God we must exercise all the wisdom we have. We can do immense damage to others and to God's cause if we lack maturity. Many such words are given to help and direct intercession and not for public broadcasting. Patience and wisdom always go together. Sin and haste are common partners.

Gift of Faith

This doesn't refer to the ordinary faith, our commitment to Christ, but to a special gift of faith. Knowing that God will act or a certain thing will happen. Praying for the seemingly impossible. As Jesus stood at the tomb of Lazarus he had the gift of faith. There was no doubt in his heart that God was about to raise the dead.

Gift of Healing

This gift is when we obey Jesus' command to lay hands on the sick (Mark 16:18), and we see them recover. Sometimes immediately, sometimes later on, sometimes only after persistent prayer.

Gift of Miracles

The feeding of the 5,000, Moses parting the Red Sea. These are miracles. The Holy Spirit gives the ability to do miracles. This gift sometimes overlaps with Faith and Healing. I remember some years ago standing with two friends in the middle of a jungle in the Philippines. Three hundred people turned out to meet us and hear us preach. Only seven of them were Christian. At the end of the meeting 250 people had committed their lives to Christ. Some people brought to us an old man who was completely blind. "You said Jesus heals people, please heal this man," was the blunt request. We looked at each other and saw the opposite of faith in each other's face. In obedience to God we prayed and asked God to heal this man. The man said he could now see light and dark but nothing else. We prayed again. Now he said he could see people but not make out their faces. We prayed again. "I can see" he said. Even then I wasn't wholly convinced. Two years later, visiting the Philippines again, the local pastor told us that not only were all those 250 people still part of the church, but that blind man could still see and was leading a normal life. We may not have had much faith, but the blind man did. So the Gifts of Faith, Healing and Miracles worked together to glorify God.

Gift of Prophecy

Prophecy is sometimes thought of as foretelling the future. There may be an element of that, but it is more concerned with telling forth the word of God. It is not preaching, nor a skill of analysing political developments. Prophecy is a message direct from God for the building up of the Church.

Being given a message of prophecy does not make you superior to the leaders of the Church. All prophecy must be tested by the leaders of the Church. The prophet's task ends with the delivery of the prophecy to Church leaders. It may be written or spoken. Some churches seem to attract a number of aspiring prophets who see complicated visions which are hard to comprehend. However, Paul says in 1 Corinthians 14:29 that only three at the maximum should speak.

Prophecy is for three things, *"... strengthening, encouragement and comfort."* (1 Corinthians 14:3). If you constantly feel the need to harangue your leaders with messages of doom and calamity, it probably isn't the gift of prophecy you have, but the gift of discouragement, which is not from God at all.

Gift of Discernment

Sometimes referred to as *"distinguishing between spirits"*, this is needed to discern prophecy which may be true or false. This gift is also helpful when confronted with evil spirits.

Gift of Tongues

To speak fluently in a language not learned. It may be a human language or an angelic language, (1 Corinthians 13:1). Mainly for use in private. Helpful for when we just don't know what to pray. Praying in tongues builds the Christian up, *"He who speaks in a tongue edifies himself, ..."* (1 Corinthians 14:4). It may also be used occasionally in public worship but Paul says it is better then if there is an interpretation. We may speak in tongues and sing in tongues (1 Corinthians 14:15).

Gift of Interpretation

This gift is when God gives the interpretation of a tongue spoken in worship, usually to a different person than the person who spoke in tongues. Together these two gifts have a similar purpose to prophecy.

All these gifts are given to build up the body of Christ, the Church.

All fall down?

There is some anxiety today, about the increasingly common experience of falling over in the Spirit. Often this happens when we are being prayed for with the laying on of hands. This experience certainly happened in the Bible. When Daniel had a vision of God he describes his condition, *"... I had no strength left, my face turned deathly pale and I was helpless... I fell into a deep sleep, my face to the ground. ... trembling on my hands and knees."* (Daniel 10:8-10).

When armed soldiers arrived to arrest Jesus they fell in his presence, *"When Jesus said, "I am he," they drew back and fell to the ground."* (John 18:6). John on the island of Patmos reacted to the overwhelming presence of Jesus in a similar way, *"When I saw him, I fell at his feet as though dead..."* (Revelation 1:17).

It seems that when some people come into God's presence, their bodies totally relax and they fall to the ground. To an onlooker this may seem very distressing - as though those who prayed had some supernatural power to make people faint. But those who fall over don't lose consciousness and are normally able to get up when they want to. Some people describe this experience as *'spending a little time with God'*, or *'Like being wrapped in pink cotton wool'*, or *'God just took all my worries away'*.

Unfortunately, there has been a wrong connection made between this experience and God's blessing. Certainly, God seems to bless those who fall over. However, it is not true that God withholds his blessing or healing from those who don't fall over. Most of the people Jesus healed in the gospels did not fall over.

It is even more unfortunate that some leaders of meetings are so keen that anyone prayed for must fall over, that accusations of, 'He pushed me over', are not uncommon. I cannot stress too much that God's healing or blessing is in no way dependent on a person falling over. It's a shame that such controversy accompanies this experience in some places, because when it happens naturally, it is a most wonderful experience. God sometimes uses this phenomenon to anoint people for a particular ministry or service.

The Sovereign Spirit

Above all the Holy Spirit must be sovereign in the life of the Christian. We must let him have full sway in our lives. We need not fear. He will not make us strange or warp our personality, indeed he may even straighten us out a bit! The Fruit of the Spirit is self control, so he will not make us lose control against our will. The Holy Spirit is not an evil spirit, so he will not possess us to do evil. Jesus said, *"If you then, though you are evil, know how to give good gifts to your children, how much more will your Father in heaven give the Holy Spirit to those who ask him!"* (Luke 11:13).

Test the Spirits

"Dear friends, do not believe every spirit, but test the spirits to see whether they are from God, because many false prophets have gone out into the world. This is how you can recognise the Spirit of God: Every spirit that acknowledges that Jesus Christ has come in the flesh is from God, but every spirit that does not acknowledge Jesus is not from God..." (1 John 4:1-3).

When God does anything beautiful, the devil will offer a counterfeit. Here is the acid test. The Holy Spirit leads nowhere but to Jesus. He points us to the cross, he convicts us of sin, he calls us to love others and go the second mile. Spiritual activity which glorifies Jesus is likely to be of God. That which distracts us from Jesus is not of God.

For this reason, it is well worth examining your life before you ask for the Holy Spirit. As far as it is up to you, rid yourself of all spiritual impurity. Where you have allowed evil a foothold, you must now renounce it.

If you have ever been involved in any of the following, you need to renounce them completely: Horoscopes, Ouija Boards, Seances, calling on the dead, Yoga, Tarot Cards, I Ching, Freemasonry, Witchcraft, Magic Arts, Astral Projection, Hypnotism, belief in Reincarnation, the Occult. Burn any books or equipment you have which relate to these subjects (Acts 19:19). All these things are rooted in false religion or paganism. They are incompatible with the Holy Spirit. We are to be on first name terms with the Holy Spirit.

The Spirit of Jesus

The Holy Spirit is the very same Spirit that was at work in the life of Jesus. St Paul wrote, *"If the Spirit of him who raised Jesus from the dead is living in you, he who raised Christ from the dead will also give life to your mortal bodies through his Spirit, who lives in you."* (Romans 8:11). Think of it. The same Spirit that entered into the tomb of the dead Jesus and brought about his amazing resurrection, can live in you! What a power! What an offer!

The Holy Spirit is for you

God offers this Holy Spirit to all Christians. Peter said, on the day of Pentecost, *"The promise is for you and your children and for all who are far off - for all whom the Lord our God will call."* (Acts 2:39). For many people, this is a subsequent experience to becoming a Christian (Acts 8:15-16; 19:1-6). For some, both conversion and baptism in the Holy Spirit seem to happen at the same time.

God wants you to be baptised in the Holy Spirit. It is not an optional extra, but full Christian life. God's word urges us to *"eagerly desire the ...gifts"* (1 Corinthians 12:31).

When you ask God to baptise you with the Holy Spirit, it is difficult to say what will happen. For some, it is like St Paul on the Damascus road, an earth-shattering event. To others, the Holy Spirit comes so quietly it takes a while to realise he has come.

When I asked God to baptise me with the Holy Spirit, it was a very quiet affair. I confessed my sin, renounced evil, and asked for the Holy Spirit. After a little while, I began to speak quietly in tongues. I was reminded of the Christmas carol which says, *"How silently, how silently the wondrous gift is given. So God imparts, to human hearts, the wonders of his heaven."* It was a quiet affair, but I've never been the same since.

God wants you to receive his most precious gift. At this point some Christians may become fearful. We are so prone to fear that the words *'Fear not'*, occur no less than 366 times in the Bible, one for every day of the year, even in a leap year! Normally this command to *'Fear not'*, came just before God did something new. So there is no need to fear. God only gives good gifts. You are so precious to him, he wants you to have his own Spirit living in your heart. Above all things, he wants you to know him intimately. This you can never do without the Holy Spirit. May I challenge you to seek God and ask him to baptise you with the Holy Spirit? You can do it very simply today.

Find a place where you can pray, or ask a Christian friend to help you pray a prayer like this.

Lord Jesus,
I thank you for dying on the cross for me.
I give my life totally to you today.
I ask you to forgive my sin ...
(mention particular things).
I renounce completely my involvement in ...
(let the Holy Spirit bring things to mind).
I ask you now to give me your gift and baptise me with the Holy Spirit.
I receive you now Holy Spirit.
Come Holy Spirit.
You are welcome.
In the name of Jesus.
Amen.

Spend a little time in quiet prayer, thanking God for his grace and goodness. Open your hands in a gesture of receiving.

If you have asked and believed, God will keep his promise. Keep thanking him for giving you the Holy Spirit, even if you don't feel different at first. We only receive baptism in the Holy Spirit once, for all time. However, we need to ask God to fill us with his Holy Spirit over and over again, everyday, as we face certain situations and tasks. The formula is simple: one baptism, many fillings, constant anointing. As you grow in the fellowship of the Holy Spirit, remember the point of it: *"The manifestation of the Spirit is given for the common good"* (1 Corinthians 12:7). This experience will not solve all your problems, but it will add a new dimension of power and joy to your life which you never thought possible. May God bless you abundantly, as you discover for yourself the beauty and grace of the Holy Spirit.

4. Blood Brothers

You are part of an ancient covenant that was designed to bring blessing into your life, and through you, into the lives of others.

When I first became a Christian, our church used to sing a chorus about the blood of Jesus:

O the blood of Jesus.
O the blood of Jesus.
O the blood of Jesus.
It washes white as snow.

There were other songs we sang which made mention of the blood of Jesus. At that time, I didn't really understand the significance of the blood of Jesus, but I knew the power of God was often released as we gave reverence to the blood of Jesus Christ. As I have studied this subject over the years, I have made an incredible discovery. It's a discovery that has revolutionised my thinking and my life. I hope you will catch this revelation as you read these words, so that you may *"...be transformed by the renewing of your mind..."* (Romans 12:2).

To begin our discovery we have to go back thousands of years, way before Jesus walked on the earth. We begin in the book of Genesis when God began a special relationship with a man called Abram, who later became Abraham. Abraham's father, Terah, had served other gods (Joshua 24:2). So when Abram began to discover the Living God, it is probable that he mixed some of his occult practices with his worship of the true God. Because of this, God was not able to bless Abram as much as he wanted to. So he called Abram to leave his people and to purify himself from the corrupt practices of the occult.

"Now the Lord had said to Abram:
"Get out of your country,
From your family

And from your father's house,
To a land that I will show you.
I will make you a great nation;
I will bless you
And make your name great;
And you shall be a blessing.
I will bless those who bless you,
And I will curse him who curses you;
And in you all the families of the earth shall be blessed."
(Genesis 12:1-3).

Here, God declares a blessing on Abraham - that he will be *blessed to be a blessing.* Some people want to be blessed but they're not interested in being a blessing to others. Some people want to bless others but don't think they should receive any blessing themselves. But God declares a very balanced thing over Abram - *be blessed in order to be a blessing.* It was such a blessing that he was to receive, that it has touched my family thousands of years later. God said, *"And in you all the families of the earth shall be blessed."* My family is one of the families of the earth, so we are blessed in Abraham.

Now Abram had a problem. He had no children. So when God gave him a vision about being blessed, Abram cried out from the pain in his soul.

"Then Abram said, "Look, You have given me no offspring!" (Genesis 15:3). God took him outside into the dark night and told him to look at the stars. He said his children would be more numerous than the stars of the sky. Against all the odds, Abram believed him. But God didn't stop there; he now spoke about the promised land. The blessing he wanted to give Abram was much more than Abram could have imagined or asked for.

"Then He said to him, "I am the Lord, who brought you out of Ur of the Chaldeans, to give you this land to inherit it." And he said, "Lord GOD, how shall I know that I will inherit it?"

So He said to him, "Bring Me a three-year-old heifer, a three-year-old female goat, a three-year-old ram, a turtledove, and a young pigeon." Then he brought all these to Him and cut them in two, down the middle, and placed each piece opposite the other; but he did not cut the birds in two." (Genesis 15:7-10).

To our Western mind this seems very odd. Abram says, *'How can I know what you say is true?'* and God seems to want to open a butcher's shop?! However, Abram knew exactly what God was doing - he was establishing a blood covenant.

The nearest thing we have in our European culture is a legal document. Yet that really pales into insignificance next to a blood covenant, because these days legal documents have so many 'get out' clauses.

A marriage is also a covenant - intended to make two people one for life. Two families become joined together. The strengths of the husband can cancel out certain weaknesses in the wife. The strengths of the wife can cancel out certain weaknesses in the husband. The two together are stronger than the individuals separately. But a blood covenant is even more than this.

In the days of Abraham, it was customary to make a blood covenant in certain situations. Let us take, for example, the case of two families. Family number one are farmers. Let's call them the Giles family. The Giles family are very skilled farmers and reap larger harvests than any of their neighbours. But they have a problem. People keep stealing their crops. Unfortunately, they are useless at fighting and are completely unable to defend their property. People just walk all over them.

Now here's family number two. They are warriors. Let's call them the Rambo family. They are very good at fighting. There is no one who can stand against them. But they also have a problem. They don't know how to farm the ground. They can't produce the food they need to eat, so they never have enough food.

Then, one day, the elders of these two families begin to discuss a covenant. The families meet together to negotiate terms. When all the negotiations are done, they meet again to make a covenant. All the members of both families are required to attend, to witness the covenant. An animal is sacrificed by cutting it in two. The pieces are laid opposite one another, so the ground between is covered in blood. Then the elders of each family cut their hand so that their blood flows. Then they join hands with the other elder and their blood mingles together as they stand in the blood of the sacrificed animal. As they recite the agreement, they walk in the blood together, in front of all the witnesses. The two families now become one family. The farmers give the fighters their best farming tool. The fighters give the farmers their best weapon. They say, *'Everything we have is yours. Everything you have is ours.'* The agreement is sworn in blood. The covenant can never be broken.

Now the fighting power of the warriors becomes the power and security of the farmers. Never again will they suffer attack. The farming skills of the farmers become the provision of the fighters. Never again will they suffer lack and hunger. The weaknesses of each family are cancelled out by the strength of the ones they have come into covenant with. The two families are now one family. They are now very powerful and secure because of the covenant between them.

Now this is what God was doing with Abraham. *"And it came to pass, when the sun went down and it was dark, that behold, there appeared a smoking oven and a burning torch that passed between those pieces. On the same day the Lord made a covenant with Abram, saying: "To your descendants I have given this land..."* (Genesis 15:17,18). The *'smoking oven and a burning torch that passed between those pieces'* was the presence of the Living God. Just as the people in Moses' time would be led by the pillar of fire and cloud, so this was the manifestation of God walking in the blood to affirm his covenant with Abraham.

Now what did he promise to Abraham? Firstly, he answered his prayer for a son. But he went much further than that. He promised him that a whole nation would be descended from him, and that they would come into their own land which God now promised them. From this time, Abraham increased in every area of his life to become one of the richest people on the face of the earth. So many blessings flowed out of this covenant with God that it is impossible to mention them all. But the covenant between God and Abraham can be summed up in one phrase - *'blessed to be a blessing'*. That was the effect of the covenant for Abraham. He became incredibly blessed in every area of his life, and through him all the families of the earth are blessed.

Now you may ask, *'What has all that got to do with me today?'* Good question. Well, if we continue our study, we will see that it has everything to do with you and me today. Let us read what Paul wrote to the Galatians. *"Christ has redeemed us from the curse of the law ... that the blessing of Abraham might come upon the Gentiles in Christ Jesus, that we might receive the promise of the Spirit through faith."* (Galatians 3:13,14). Christ redeemed us from the curse. The curse of sin and death. Why? Just so we could go to heaven? Well, it includes that. But this verse says Jesus redeemed us... *"that the blessing of Abraham might come upon the Gentiles in Christ Jesus..."* Now when Jesus died on the cross he was fully God and fully man. When that blood ran down his body, the blood of God and the blood of man was mingled together making a blood covenant between man and God. Not only that, it was also a covenant that brought everyone who is in Christ - the Christian born-again believer - into the blessing of Abraham. Jesus spoke plainly about this at the last supper, when he foreshadowed his death on the cross by speaking about the bread and the wine as his body and his blood.

"Then He took the cup, and when He had given thanks He gave it to them, and they all drank from it. And He said to them, "This is My blood of the new covenant, which is shed for many." (Mark 14:23-24).

Once we grasp this understanding of how Jesus brought us into a special covenant relationship, then we begin to understand that we no longer have to live in any kind of poverty whether of health, spirit, or finances or anything else. When I married Hazel, my wife, we came into a covenant with each other. In the wedding service, I said to her *"All that I am I give to you. All that I have I share with you, within the love of God."* She said the same to me. Over the years we have been a great blessing to each other because of that covenant we made.

However, God's covenant with the believer is much more powerful than that. Let's look again at the story of the lost son (Luke 15:11). It's one most of us know. The son takes half his father's wealth and wastes it all on wild living. When it has all gone he finds himself in trouble.

Hungry and poor, and living in a pig sty, he decides to return home and at least get a job on his father's farm. However, his father welcomes him back with open arms and throws a party to celebrate the return of his lost and wayward son. That, of course, is a picture of a lost sinner returning home to the Father. But Jesus' story goes on to tell of the older brother. He was furious that his father should give anything to his brother, let alone throw an extravagant party for him. He said, *"...these many years I have been serving you; I never transgressed your commandment at any time; and yet you never gave me a young goat, that I might make merry with my friends."* (Luke 15:29).

You never gave me anything. That was his complaint. That's the cry of many believers today, especially when they see anyone being blessed by God, and especially when they see anyone financially blessed by God. Jealousy rises up within them.

'You never gave me anything!' They think it, even if most don't say it.

What does the father say in reply? *"Son, you are always with me, and all that I have is yours."* (Luke 15:31). He says what I said to my wife on our wedding day. *'All that I have is yours.'* When God says that to us, it is really mind boggling. All he has is mine. All I have is his. I think I got the better deal there. When I came into a relationship with God, I brought certain things with me. So did he. I brought sin - he brought forgiveness. I brought sickness - he brought healing. I brought poverty - he brought provision. I brought hopelessness - he brought hope. I brought darkness - he brought light. I brought a tendency to sin - he brought a tendency to holiness.

Why is it then, that so many Christians live with a spirit of poverty, with sickness and small-mindedness. They're like the older brother who remained faithful but didn't realise he could claim what belonged to his father, so he could be blessed to be a blessing. What so many people just can't get hold of is why God would want to bless them. What have they done to deserve it? Well, nothing, that's the whole point. The covenant speaks of God's generosity, not our worthiness. Psalm 35:27 says, *"the Lord... has pleasure in the prosperity of His servant."* It gives God great pleasure to see people receive increased blessing in every area of their life.

Let's look at another example of a covenant where the blessing seems so one-way. In 2 Samuel 9 we read about a man called Mephibosheth. He was a cripple and descended from David's predecessor, Saul. Mephibosheth lived in a place called Lo Debar, which literally means 'the place of no pasture'. In 1 Samuel 20 David enters into a covenant with Jonathan, Saul's son. And this covenant not only applied to them, but to their descendants also.

"And Jonathan said to David, "Come, and let us go out into

the field." So both of them went out into the field. Then Jonathan said to David: "The Lord God of Israel is witness! ...And you shall not only show me the kindness of the Lord while I still live, that I may not die; but you shall not cut off your kindness from my house forever, no, not when the Lord has cut off every one of the enemies of David from the face of the earth." So Jonathan made a covenant with the house of David, saying, "Let the Lord require it at the hand of David's enemies." Now Jonathan again caused David to vow, because he loved him; for he loved him as he loved his own soul." (1 Samuel 20:11-17).

Jonathan wanted to protect David from being killed, but he went much further by entering into a mutually beneficial covenant, one which would also bless their descendants. So, some time later, David remembered his covenant with Jonathan and looked to see if their was anyone still living who would be a beneficiary.

"Now David said, "Is there still anyone who is left of the house of Saul, that I may show him kindness for Jonathan's sake?" (2 Samuel 9:1).

The only one was Mephibosheth. So Mephibosheth came from the desert place into the king's presence. He must have been amazed as he heard the announcement of the king. He certainly felt unworthy of such blessing.

"Then [Mephibosheth] bowed himself, and said, "What is your servant, that you should look upon such a dead dog as I?" (2 Samuel 9:8).

But David had in mind the terms of the covenant, not the condition of the beneficiary.

So David said to him, *"Do not fear, for I will surely show you kindness for Jonathan your father's sake, and will restore to you all the land of Saul your grandfather; and you shall eat bread at my table continually."* (2 Samuel 9:7).

"As for Mephibosheth," said the king, *"he shall eat at my table like one of the king's sons."* (2 Samuel 9:11).

What happened to Mephibosheth is a perfect picture of God's dealings with men and women. Crippled by sin and fear, we live out our days in a very dry and lonely place. But the King has summoned us to the palace. When we come to him, he declares such a blessing over us that we can hardly take it in. We can't believe that the King wants us to eat at his table and restore to us everything that has been taken from us.

When I began to claim the things Jesus paid for me to have with his own blood, there was a backlash. We do have an enemy in the devil. He is the one who has stolen our health, our provision and our peace. Jesus called our enemy a thief. *"The thief does not come except to steal, and to kill, and to destroy. I have come that they may have life, and that they may have it more abundantly."* (John 10:10).

After forty years of believing the devil's lies and allowing him to steal my health, my provision, my peace and all that Jesus paid for me to have, he isn't going to give up things without a fight. However, also included in the blood of Jesus is total victory over all the powers of darkness. Jesus has not only paid for me to live in abundance, but he has also won the victory over the enemy and paid for the faith and wisdom I need to achieve the abundant life.

Jesus wanted you to be included in the new covenant and used his own blood in paying for you to be abundantly provided for. He wants you to be blessed to be a blessing. The blood of Jesus has paid for your healing. The blood of Jesus has paid for your peace. The blood of Jesus has paid for your sin. The blood of Jesus has paid for you to have all your needs met according to his riches in glory. The blood of Jesus has paid for you to be blessed to be a blessing. Search his last will and testament. The New Testament in the Bible is actually the

New Covenant. Search his word to find what he has promised for you, and then start claiming what is rightfully yours in Jesus.

5. I have a dream...

One of the most moving film clips I know is that of Martin Luther King Jr.'s sermon, 'I have a dream...'

"I say to you today, my friends, that in spite of the difficulties and frustrations of the moment, I still have a dream. It is a dream deeply rooted in the American dream.

I have a dream that one day this nation will rise up and live out the true meaning of its creed: "We hold these truths to be self-evident: that all men are created equal."

I have a dream that one day on the red hills of Georgia the sons of former slaves and the sons of former slaveowners will be able to sit down together at a table of brotherhood.

I have a dream that one day even the state of Mississippi, a desert state, sweltering with the heat of injustice and oppression, will be transformed into an oasis of freedom and justice.

I have a dream that my four children will one day live in a nation where they will not be judged by the colour of their skin but by the content of their character.

I have a dream today. I have a dream that one day the state of Alabama, whose governor's lips are presently dripping with the words of interposition and nullification, will be transformed into a situation where little black boys and black girls will be able to join hands with little white boys and white girls and walk together as sisters and brothers.

I have a dream today.

I have a dream that one day every valley shall be exalted, every hill and mountain shall be made low, the rough places will be made plain, and the crooked places will be made straight, and the glory of the Lord shall be revealed, and all flesh shall see it together.

This is our hope. This is the faith with which I return to the South. With this faith we will be able to hew out of the mountain of despair a stone of hope. With this faith we will be able to transform the jangling discords of our nation into a beautiful symphony of brotherhood. With this faith we will be able to work together, to pray together, to struggle together, to go to jail together, to stand up for freedom together, knowing that we will be free one day."

(Speech by Martin Luther King Jr. Delivered on the steps at the Lincoln Memorial in Washington D.C. on August 28, 1963).

Martin Luther King was later assassinated by those trying to destroy the civil rights movement in America.

I am moved by his words. Not only because he was right in his struggle, but because, like most of us, I too, have a dream. I am moved by Martin Luther King because he chased his dream, made sacrifices to achieve his dream, and eventually paid the ultimate price to bring his dream about. The world is a different place today because of the dream-chasers.

Many people have a dream today, but they don't pursue it. They're not willing to pay the price to bring it about. People talk at great length about their dream or their vision. Yet, when everything is said and done, there is a lot more said than done. They grow old and spend their days asking themselves 'What if...?' But you don't need to do that. You can have a dream, and you can see it come to be a reality, as you grow in your love of God. The Bible says, *"Delight yourself in the Lord and he will give you the desires of your heart."* (Psalms 37:4).

Many people in the churches today are interested in preserving history, to such an extent that it can even hinder the work of the Kingdom of God. Denominations and churches are often founded by an outstanding man. The work of that man creates a movement. And when he dies the movement becomes a monument to his memory, devoid of all the dynamism of the original vision. A man, a movement, a monument. And the followers gather at the grave of the vision and perpetuate a weekly funeral service. There are so many of these groups and sometimes they meet together and talk about unity, as though gathering several corpses together might generate life. Like Lot's wife they look back and become dry, inflexible, bitter and dead. But Christians should be making history, not preserving it. We should be magnifying Jesus in all the world. After all, history is His story.

Between adolescence and our late thirties, the predominate question in our heart is 'Who am I?' If we manage to answer that one, then, by mid life, the next question is 'What should I do with my life?' If we are ever to still the restlessness in our human spirit, we need to find some answers to these deep-seated questions. We need to understand who God says we are, and to understand what his purpose is for us on this planet. To reach the full potential that God has planned for us, we have to work and to plan. You will never walk in the things God has planned for you by sitting on your blessed assurance. We have to rise up and claim our promised land.

God has a plan for you, whoever you are. *"For I know the plans I have for you," declares the Lord, plans to prosper you and not to harm you, plans to give you hope and a future."* (Jeremiah 29:11). When we become a Christian, we open the door to God's plan for us. Through Jesus Christ, God begins a new work in us as we surrender to his will. *"For we are God's workmanship, created in Christ Jesus to do good works, which God prepared in advance for us to do."* (Ephesians 2:10).

In 1980, I had dream. It was a strange dream, through which God began to speak to me about his plan for my life. It was a call to full-time ministry and a call to preach in other nations. Almost twenty years later, that vision is only just beginning to become established. There have been years of preparation, battles and frustrations, years of character building and learning from God and from others. Many times I have felt like giving up. At other times I felt I was wasting my time.

I remember a day when I was at college, training for ministry. The first task of the day was 'scrubology'. I was given a polishing machine and told to polish the vast floor in the college dining room. It took hours and I lost myself in a private world skidding championship on the well-polished floor. Hours were also spent drinking coffee and debating answers to questions that no one was asking. Some afternoons I sat with a badly constructed essay on my desk, looking out of the window, watching the rain outside, and wondering what had happened to the dream of ministry.

Even when we got to do some ministry, it seemed a far cry from what God had called me to do. During a college mission, I was sent to stay with the church organist. She was a grey-haired lady who appeared to have applied her lipstick during an earth tremor. In the kitchen she introduced me to Plantagenet, a large cockerel who had fallen out of a tree and broken its leg. The leg, now in plaster, was slowly mending. So he wandered about the kitchen every morning, looking at me suspiciously as I consumed my cornflakes. In the evening, my host announced that she always watched the Miss Marple series on TV. Actually, she looked a bit like Miss Marple, but was slightly more eccentric. It was obvious that I was not to speak during the programme, so I sat trying to look interested and wondered, again, if the dream of God's call on my life would ever come to be.

But those were days of sifting. It's important to know what God has *not* called you to, as well as what he *has* called you to. Many people feel that they have been knitting with fog for most of their life, and it is good to discover what we're not. Wherever possible though, we should avoid time wasting and examine the opportunities before us, to see if they are going to help or prevent us reaching our goal. And here's the problem - many of us don't have a goal. If we aim at nothing, that is what we will achieve.

Walt Disney died before the official opening of Disney World in Florida. At the opening ceremony the speaker said, "I wish Walt could have seen this!" Behind him, Walt Disney's wife whispered, "He did!"

A vision is seeing something that others don't see and believing that you can bring it into being. The vision will only come about through the power and blessing of God as we walk in the Spirit. The one who gives the vision also gives the provision - everything we need to bring the vision into being.

We need to get the vision for our life. We need to get it from God. God is more than willing to reveal his will for your life and you don't need to be super-spiritual to receive it. Jesus said, *"I thank You, Father, Lord of heaven and earth, that You have hidden these things from the wise and prudent and revealed them to babes. Even so, Father, for so it seemed good in Your sight."* (Luke 10:21). God is willing to give you the revelation of his will for your life. *"There is a God in heaven who reveals mysteries..."* (Daniel 2:28). Even a pagan king recognised God's will is to give people revelation. *"The king said to Daniel, "Surely your God is the God of gods and the Lord of kings and a revealer of mysteries..."* (Daniel 2:47). James 1:5 says, *"If any of you lacks wisdom, he should ask God, who gives generously to all without finding fault, and it will be given to him."* (James 1:5).

When we get the vision, we need to write it down. *"Write the vision and make it plain on tablets, that he may run who reads it."* (Habakkuk 2:2). One of the obstacles to understanding the vision God has for you, is a failure to write down thoughts and words from God and from yourself. My first real break-through in bringing about my vision, came when I started putting pen to paper. This makes the vision clear. It clarifies it in our own mind and in the minds of others. As others have read and understood the vision I have, they have been able to run with it, to join me in that vision. The best place to begin is by having a notebook which records a dialogue with God. I have a note-book which I take with me when I pray each morning. Some days I don't write anything down. Some days I have an inspired thought. Some days it seems God speaks to me through his word in the Bible. As I write God's personal word to me, a picture begins to develop. As I review all these words after a period of time, the vision becomes clearer. There is a flow which shows me the bigger picture of God's will for my life.

Some years ago, God spoke to me about the future. I was praying about the present. and complaining about the past. I believe God led me to write my vision in just two sentences at the top of a piece of paper. At the bottom of the paper, he led me to write down where I was at the moment. In the middle of the paper I made two columns. On the left I wrote down all the obstacles to getting from the present situation at the bottom of the paper, to the vision at the top of the paper. On the right I wrote a list of people who could help me get to the top of the paper. I then turned the paper over and listed several steps I would have to take to bring the vision into being. Some things could be done immediately; others would take months or years. But I made a quality decision that day, to take all the necessary steps to bring about the vision. Every journey begins with the first step. I kept that paper and referred back to it every few months to assess my progress under God. I wrote further plans and steps I needed to take. I dreamt dreams and made plans.

Many Christians don't like making plans. *"I'm just trusting the Holy Spirit."* they say, sounding very spiritual. Well, God gave us a brain, and that's one of the things the Holy Spirit uses to help us bring about God's plan for our life. If we are walking in the Spirit and putting Jesus first above all things, his Spirit in us will help us make godly plans. The Bible says,

"The plans of the righteous are just, but the advice of the wicked is deceitful." (Proverbs 12:5).

"Do not those who plot evil go astray? But those who plan what is good find love and faithfulness." (Proverbs 14:22).

"Commit to the Lord whatever you do, and your plans will succeed." (Proverbs 16:3).

"In his heart a man plans his course, but the Lord determines his steps." (Proverbs 16:9).

"Many are the plans in a man's heart, but it is the Lord's purpose that prevails." (Proverbs 19:21).

"Make plans by seeking advice; if you wage war, obtain guidance." (Proverbs 20:18).

"The plans of the diligent lead to profit as surely as haste leads to poverty" (Proverbs 21:5).

As we get the vision and make our plans, led by the Spirit of God, we will almost certainly face obstacles. Some seem difficult to get over and we can become frustrated. We may feel like giving up, but we mustn't. Winston Churchill's shortest speech is said to have been made at a university. Thousands gathered to hear the wisdom of this wartime leader. He stood at the lectern and said, *"Never give up! Never give up! Never give up!"* Then he sat down and got a standing ovation. Many of the great heroes of the Bible were frustrated in one way or another but they pressed on through the problems and won the victory.

Abraham was childless but God gave him a vision to be the father of many nations. In frustration, he tried to help God out when the vision seemed to be taking too long. He slept with a servant girl who gave him a child, but this was not the child of promise. Eventually, Isaac was born, just as God had said.

After murdering an Egyptian, Moses spent forty years in the wilderness as a shepherd, before he led his people out of slavery. David, the shepherd boy, had the anointing to be king but not the crown. He went through many trials and frustrations before he took the throne. You may be in a situation now where you feel you have the anointing but not the crown. God says to you, "Don't give up!"

Sometimes a delay is necessary for us to develop our character and our integrity. If we are going into the woods to chop down trees, the time we take to sharpen our axe will not be wasted. God will not do a great work through you until he has done a great work in you. To achieve anything great we have to stand our ground in the face of trouble and press on towards the victory. St Paul wrote, *"One thing I do: Forgetting what is behind and straining towards what is ahead, I press on towards the goal to win the prize for which God has called me heavenwards in Christ Jesus."* (Philippians 3:13,14). And in the midst of all the battles that may come our way, we mustn't allow ourselves to get bitter about the past. The Bible says, *"See to it that ... no bitter root grows up to cause trouble and defile many."* (Hebrews 12:15).

In more recent history, we find stories of people who have pressed through and overcome incredible difficulties, in order to bring about their vision. Lord Nelson suffered from sea sickness all his life - but he refused to let his personal struggles rob him of his destiny.

Charles Darrow brought the first prototype of the board game Monopoly to Parker Brothers in 1934. They laughed him out of the office saying, *"That's a really stupid game. It's never going to sell. It's far too complicated. It takes far too long to play. We are experts on games and we figure that there are 52 major flaws in this game of Monopoly."* But that did not deter Charles Darrow. He began to market the game on his own. Within one year, one department store sold 5,000 sets. It was such a success Parker Brothers confessed, "Maybe we were a little too hasty." They signed a contract with Charles Darrow and he became a multi-millionaire. They have since sold 100 million sets of Monopoly in 54 countries and in 26 languages. More than 3.2 billion little green houses have been produced. If you took all those little green houses and put them side by side, they would encircle the whole earth.

James Dyson noticed that most vacuum cleaners lose suction after only one room because the pores in the bag clog with dust. It took him 5 years, hundreds of thousands of pounds of debts, several lawsuits and 5,127 prototypes to produce the world's first bagless vacuum cleaner. He was constantly told, *"If there was a better way to design a vacuum cleaner, Hoover would have done it by now."* The Dyson DC01 vacuum cleaner is now the best selling vacuum cleaner in the world with sales of over £2 billion worldwide.

If we are going to bring about the fruit of our vision, we will have to develop patience.

In the parable of the sower Jesus said, *"But the ones that fell on the good ground are those who, having heard the word with a noble and good heart, keep it and bear fruit with patience."* (Luke 8:15). Luke 21:19 says, *"By your patience possess your souls."*

Hebrews 6:12 says, *"...do not become sluggish, but imitate those who through faith and patience inherit the promises."* James 1:4 says, *"But let patience have its perfect work, that you may be perfect and complete, lacking nothing."* Let us not despise the day a small things (Zechariah 4:10).

So if you have a dream:

1. Get your vision from God - it will agree with his word. (James 1:5).

2. Write it down. List all the obstacles you can think of. List all those things or people who can help you with your vision.

3. Set goals and make plans and strategies.

4. Take all the steps needed to bring the vision about. Some you can do today. Others will take time - so set a date for them.

5. Be persistent and be patient, as the vision grows and comes into being.

6. Constantly review your plans and adapt them to the situation.

6. Avoid Organ Recitals

I used to belong to a prayer meeting where we prayed for the sick. Well, we were supposed to pray for the sick, but we tended to get organ recitals instead. It went something like this, *"Lord, we pray for Bill who has lung cancer. Lord, we pray for Gertrude who has failed kidneys. Lord, we pray for Fred with a bad heart. Lord, we pray for Sally with a damaged liver...."*

And so it went on. We didn't pray in faith, because we focussed on the diseased organs not on the Healer. We recited a list of organs - we had our own organ recital. We committed the mistake of the Israelites when faced with Goliath - we looked at the problem instead of the power of God. David defeated Goliath because he focussed on God's power and his word, not on the Goliath-size problem.

If you want to be healed, or to be used by God to heal others, then you need to learn what God says about healing. You need to focus on his word rather than the problem. You need to remove from your mind and heart all the lies about healing that you may have accepted by basing your understanding of healing on opinion, speculation and the devil's lies.

In the story of the prodigal son there are three characters who all teach us something about God and ourselves. The main character is the father, who loves both his sons equally, even though one is a prodigal and one is a faithful hard worker. If you are looking for healing, the key to your good health is in this story. When the prodigal had spent all the father had given him, he devised a plan to come back into his father's blessing, albeit in a reduced way.

He said, *"I will arise and go to my father, and will say to him, "Father, I have sinned against heaven and before you, and I am no longer worthy to be called your son. Make me like one of your hired servants."* (Luke 15:18,19).

He had left home as a son and now he thought he could go back as a stranger and a servant. This is the condition of everyone who has not received Jesus Christ into their heart as their Saviour. His decision to go home humbly repenting was the key to his restoration. The Bible describes the condition of people without Jesus. *"At that time you were without Christ, being aliens from the commonwealth of Israel and strangers from the covenants of promise, having no hope and without God in the world."* (Ephesians 2:12).

This son had become a stranger to the relationship with his father and was without hope in the world. He lived in a pig sty and he was eating pig swill. Spiritually speaking, many people are in a pig sty eating pig swill, and they wonder why they are dissatisfied with life. Sadly, many people in churches are living in a pigsty of broken faith and eating a daily diet of pig swill - doctrines of tradition made by men which have no biblical foundation.

The teaching that God may send sickness upon a person to teach them something, has held many believers bound up with sickness and disease unnecessarily. That teaching is from the pit of hell. God is good. He wants you healed. He would never send a sickness upon you. God is good all the time. If God is trying to teach you something by making you sick, how dare you go to the doctor and try to get well! The idea that God wants you sick so you learn a little lesson is utter pig swill. Jesus himself carried our sickness so we don't have to. *"He Himself took our infirmities and bore our sicknesses."* Matthew 8:17.

When he went back to his father, the son in the story was not accepted as a servant, but was fully restored as a son. He came back into the position his elder brother had occupied all the time. But his elder brother didn't understand his own position and therefore failed to benefit from the blessing of being with the father. When he saw all the gifts the father was giving to his younger brother, he was resentful and started complaining.

"These many years I have been serving you; I never transgressed your commandment at any time; and yet you never gave me a young goat, that I might make merry with my friends." (Luke 15:29).

He had been faithful to the father but hadn't seen any blessing from his faithfulness. This is the feeling of so many Christians today. But what did the father say in reply? *"...all that I have is yours."* (Luke 15:31).

As far as the Father is concerned, all he has is ours. That is a covenant statement. As far as Jesus is concerned, there is little difference between forgiving sin and healing sickness. It is all part of the package. Even the English language implies this connection. The word *'salvation'* which we associate with forgiveness of sin, is from the same root as the word *'salve'* which we associate with antiseptic and healing.

In Mark chapter 2, four men break open the roof and let down a paralysed man in front of Jesus. *"When Jesus saw their faith, He said to the paralytic, "Son, your sins are forgiven you."* (Mark 2:5). But those present were offended by Jesus' words. He contradicted their tradition and they hadn't received the revelation about who Jesus was and is. Jesus said it didn't really matter whether he said 'you are forgiven', or 'you are healed'. It's all part of the package of salvation.

"But immediately, when Jesus perceived in His spirit that they reasoned thus within themselves, He said to them, "Why do you reason about these things in your hearts? "Which is easier, to say to the paralytic, `Your sins are forgiven you,' or to say, `Arise, take up your bed and walk'? "But that you may know that the Son of Man has power on earth to forgive sins" - He said to the paralytic, "I say to you, arise, take up your bed, and go to your house." Immediately he arose, took up the bed,

and went out in the presence of them all, so that all were amazed and glorified God, saying, "We never saw anything like this!"" (Mark 2:8-12).

When Jesus healed the sick he didn't pray for them. Instead, he spoke to sick bodies and commanded them to be healed, or declared that they were healed. He told this man who could not stand up, to stand up and walk home. He took authority over the man's body when he saw the faith of the four men who brought him. He said to the waves and the storm on the lake *"Peace, be still!"* (Mark 4:39). And it was still. In Mark 5:41 he spoke to a dead girl and told her to get up. And she did. In Mark 9:25 he told a deaf and dumb spirit to come out of a boy. And it did. He taught the disciples to do the same. To speak to sick bodies and command them to be healed, and expect them to be healed.

You see when God created the world, he used his word. In Genesis 1, he spoke to the darkness and said, "Let there be light." And there was light. He made us in his image and gave us dominion over the earth. Restored believers have the power and authority to speak to the natural world in accordance with God's word, and expect it to obey them.

In all our ministry to the sick, this is the method I use, because this is the method Jesus and the disciples used. I believe that God has already healed people by the blood of Jesus Christ. Their healing is a foregone conclusion. I speak healing scriptures to those gathered. I speak to their bodies and command them to be healed. Hundreds have testified to healing miracles. I have lost count of the number of blind people who have received back their sight as a result of believing Jesus and his word. I have seen lame men leaping and dancing and praising God. I have seen the deaf and dumb begin to speak, people with agonising pain become completely pain free. Jesus has paid for their healing with his own blood. All we need to do is come and claim that healing. To receive God's promise we must mix our faith with God's word. *"... but the word which they heard did not profit them, not being mixed with faith in those who heard it."* (Hebrews 4:2).

Perhaps, as you read this, you are very ill or someone you know is very sick. I know it may seem impossible to believe that you, or they, could be healed. Many years ago, I watched my own parents and my own son deteriorate and die. I didn't understand that their healing had been paid for by Jesus. I didn't understand about having authority over sick bodies. I didn't understand that Satan is a determined killer (John 10:10). I didn't have faith for healing. I found it very hard to pray. The thing seemed overwhelming. All three of them died.

Eventhough I now understand more of God's word on healing, I know sickness can be overwhelming if we allow it to be. It sometimes stands like a mountain before us, overshadowing us. But Jesus said we can speak to mountains and tell them to be removed. If we believe they will move, they will. I recently received a letter from Penny who came for prayer at a healing service in East Anglia:

"I went forward for healing of S.A.D. - Seasonal Adjusted Disorder - from which I have suffered for 46 years. The symptoms are depression in the winter months. During this time the desire to just stay in bed is great. It was an enormous effort to do the simplest thing. Memory was bad, my mind was often muddled so I couldn't make the simplest decisions. I felt miserable and useless. This S.A.D. used to ruin four months of every year. It was always aggravated by a sense of guilt - because I was letting my family down. I was ashamed because I couldn't cope, and I couldn't 'snap out of it.'

When I came for healing I didn't come with great expectations. As you prayed for me, Don, you asked God that I be 'transformed by the renewing of my mind' (Rom 12:2). And I remember agreeing - "Yes, that's it!" I remember starting to laugh and being a bit surprised, as in the past I have not laughed at all - even if I thought something was funny. I can remember saying, 'It's done. Thank you.' I am now walking in the joy of the Lord, Don. Thank you for your obedience in preaching and teaching the word of God."

Jesus said, *"For assuredly, I say to you, whoever says to this mountain, `Be removed and be cast into the sea,' and does not doubt in his heart, but believes that those things he says will be done, he will have whatever he says. Therefore I say to you, whatever things you ask when you pray, believe that you receive them, and you will have them."* (Mark 11:23-24).

Now as far as I can see, Jesus was not into landscaping. He wasn't talking about moving actual mountains. He was talking about those obstacles and difficulties in our life that seem like mountains. They block our path and make it impossible for us to go forward. So how can we believe such a big thing will move when we tell it to? Well, if it is something that Jesus has already said he wants to be moved, and he's given his word, his blood, his faith, his anointing, his power and his authority, I think we can be certain it is going to move. But we have to speak faith. Jesus said, *"he will have whatever he says."* So we have to say what we want to have. This is the thing that people find most difficult because it sounds foolish. If I am filled with sickness, I have to say *'I am healed in Jesus' name.'* That is what I want and Jesus said, *"he will have whatever he says."*

Now many people see this as denying the facts. But we mustn't confuse facts with truth. The Bible contains facts and truth. Yet most facts are preceded in the Bible with the words, *'It came to pass...'* That's what facts do. They come to pass. However, God's truth is eternal. Jesus said, *"Heaven and earth will pass away, but My words will by no means pass away."* (Mark 13:31).

Now, sometimes the *fact* of sickness contradicts the *truth* about our healing. The Bible says in Matthew 8:17, *"He Himself took our infirmities and bore our sicknesses."* In 1 Peter 2:24 it says, *"by [His] stripes you were healed."* That's past tense. You see, I am not the sick trying to get well. I am the healed from whom Satan is trying to steal health.

I remember a time, a few months ago, I became so sick in my stomach. I can't ever remember being so ill. The next day I lay in bed so weak and so sick I could barely move or even speak. Nevertheless, I began to whisper the word over my body. *"By His stripes I am healed. He has borne my sicknesses. Sickness I command you in the name of Jesus to go from my body. I break your power Satan. You have no right to touch my body with sickness. I am covered by the blood of Jesus. Body, I command you to be healed in the name of Jesus."* I continued for about five minutes and then fell asleep for an hour. When I woke up, I was at full strength and there was no trace of weakness or illness at all.

Another time I had injured my back. The pain kept me awake at night for months. I went to a back specialist. He said, "Unless God does a miracle, you will have this pain for several years to come." I began speaking the word over my body and believing that God would heal me. Weeks went by with no improvement. Then one morning I was watching a Nigerian preacher on TV. When he finished preaching, he came on at the end of the programme and suddenly said, "There is someone watching today, you injured your back some months ago. God is healing you right now!" I raised my hand and said, "Yes! Amen!" Instantly, my back was healed and I have never had any trouble with it since.

Agreement is another key to your healing. The Bible says,

"Again I say to you that if two of you agree on earth concerning anything that they ask, it will be done for them by My Father in heaven." (Matthew 18:19). The preacher declared my healing by revelation of the Holy Spirit. At the moment I agreed with him, and spoke that agreement out in faith, my healing came. Remember though, for months before I had been feeding my faith with the word of God. The Bible says, *"...faith comes by hearing, and hearing by the word of God."* (Romans 10:17). As we speak the word over our bodies, faith will begin to rise up in us, because faith comes by hearing the word of God. It is by faith that we get healed.

Some people say, 'But what about those who are not healed?' They usually have some tale about a dear soul who was prayed for but died. To ask this question exposes your doubt that God's word is true. 1 Peter 2:24 says, *"by [His] stripes you were healed."* You see, we were all healed. Therefore, the truth is, we are healed. The fact may be that we are sick, but the truth is we are healed. If we claim our healing, it will come. *'Well I've prayed for people and got the whole congregation praying and they weren't healed, they died.'* Yes. I know all about that. I prayed for my mother. I prayed for my father. I prayed for my son. And they all died. But I didn't speak faith over them and I didn't claim the healing that Jesus had paid for. I wept and wailed and asked God to help, not realising in my ignorance that he had given everything necessary for them to be healed, but I didn't believe. I had my own little organ recitals about lungs, livers and hearts. Even when I prayed, I was expecting them to die. That's not faith, that's doubt. To the vast majority of people who were healed by Jesus, in the gospels, he said to them, *"Your faith has made you well."* or to Jarius he said, *"Don't be afraid only believe."* (Mark 5:36). Fortunately, for Christians, death is not the end and God is very gracious and comforts those who mourn.

You know most of us want to talk to God *about* the mountain. But Jesus didn't say that. He said speak *to* the mountain and tell it to be removed. Unless we begin to line our faith up with the word of God, we will be frustrated in the area of healing. We will be shooting in the dark, developing our own little theology of healing - *win some, lose some.* That is not what the word says. *"For all the promises of God in Him are Yes, and in Him Amen, to the glory of God through us."* 2 Corinthians 1:20. Romans 3:4 says, *"...let God be true but every man a liar..."*

We need to be careful what we say. We need to speak the word and speak faith over our bodies. Even when I am well, I recite healing scriptures to my body. I do this to store up faith for the day when attacks on my health may come. If I have been sowing the seed of the word, which produces faith, my harvest of healing will come much quicker. It will also be much more difficult for Satan to put sickness in my body in the first place.

Here is a prayer for healing. Use it every day until your healing manifests itself. Look for other healing scriptures and memorise them and speak them over your body even when you are well. Faith comes by hearing.

"Is anyone among you sick? Let him call for the elders of the church, and let them pray over him, anointing him with oil in the name of the Lord. And the prayer of faith will save the sick, and the Lord will raise him up. And if he has committed sins, he will be forgiven. Confess your trespasses to one another, and pray for one another, that you may be healed. The effective, fervent prayer of a righteous man avails much." (James 5:14-16).

PRAYER FOR HEALING

Father, I thank you that you love me
and care for me.
I thank you for sending Jesus.
Jesus, I thank you that you took my infirmities and bore my
sicknesses so I don't have to.
You are the Lord who heals me.
And I declare your word over my body now,
that by your stripes I am healed.
I declare that Satan is a liar.
That I am not the sick trying to get well, but I am the healed,
from whom Satan is trying to steal health.
I refuse you, Satan. I refuse you, sickness.
I will not have you in my body.
I submit myself to God and I resist you devil.
You have to flee from me according to God's word.
It is written, 'Resist the devil and he will flee from you.'
I resist you now in the name of Jesus.
I speak to this mountain of sickness
and I command you to leave my body in the name of Jesus.
I take authority over this body in the name of Jesus.
I break every power of sickness affecting this body now.
I receive afresh the blood of Jesus on my life.
I declare that this body belongs to Jesus.
The Anointed One and his Anointing lives in me.
I break your power, sickness, in the name of Jesus.
Body, I take authority over you in the name of Jesus,
I command you to be healed now, in Jesus' name.
Thank you, Jesus, that you have already paid for this heal-
ing on the cross.
I receive my healing now, by faith, in Jesus' name.
I am healed by his stripes. Thank you, Father.
Amen.

(Matthew 8:17, Exodus 15:26, Isaiah 53:5)

7. Gardeners' World

In recent years there has been an explosion of gardening programmes on television. Garden centres are doing record business. Everywhere, from landscape gardens to the tower block window box, people are planting things and watching them grow and multiply. We reap what we sow. If you plant an apple seed, you will get an apple tree, not a rose bush. It may take some time, but you will reap what you sow. However, this principle is not restricted to the garden. It is also true of your thoughts, words, actions, and your finances.

The Bible says, *"Do not be deceived, God is not mocked; for whatever a man sows, that he will also reap."* (Galatians 6:7).

Jesus said that the parable of the sower was the key to understanding all the other parables; it is the 'mother of all parables', *"Do you not understand this parable? How then will you understand all the parables?"* (Mark 4:13).

One seed does not produce one seed, but many seeds. A farmer may sow from a sack, but reaps the harvest in trucks. Sowing and reaping is a multiplication phenomenon. One seed produces tens, hundreds or even thousands of new seeds. Jesus said, *"I tell you the truth, unless a grain of wheat falls to the ground and dies, it remains only a single seed. But if it dies, it produces many seeds."* (John 12:24).

Our actions are seeds. They produce a harvest. Both negative and positive actions are seeds. We see men and women who have sown goodness, later being honoured by others. We see a dispute between neighbours escalate out of control as each aggressive action reaps a multiplied response. The Bible says, *"They sow the wind, and reap the whirlwind."* (Hosea 8:7).

When we sin, we also sow a seed. We allow darkness to grow in our lives. Satan dwells in darkness. When we sow the deeds of darkness, we allow Satan space in our life. Secrecy and darkness often precede sin. But when we feed on God and his word, and put it into practice, we reap a harvest of blessing. *"The one who sows to please his sinful nature, from that nature will reap destruction; the one who sows to please the Spirit, from the Spirit will reap eternal life."* (Galatians 6:8).

Our words are seeds, and they produce a harvest. Name a baby 'Stupid' and it will be. I have wept many times in the years I have been in ministry, as I have prayed with those who have had negative things spoken over them when they were young. Those negative words, in the formative years, have produced a harvest of adults filled with self-doubt and tendencies of self-abuse. I have constantly corrected anyone who has casually spoken negatively over my children. I don't mean I am against discipline for children, but I am against foolishly speaking negative words over children (and indeed, adults). When they were young, people said they were going to be 'spoiled'. They are not going to be spoiled, they are going to be blessed. People say, 'Be a devil'. No thank you.

If we believe the negative words that have been spoken to us, then those words become seeds and produce a multiplied harvest. The harvest manifests itself in people with low self-esteem. They themselves then begin to produce more seeds from their mouth, repeating what was said about them, thus sowing and reaping a constant harvest of low self-esteem. Some go on to self-abuse. Others attempt suicide. A tragic death, begun by someone planting a negative seed in the form of words, which took root in someone's heart.

I try not to believe what people say about me, but focus on what God says about me. Sadly, in the church sometimes, people speak negatively about us. One Sunday I was standing in a church at the end of the service where I'd preached. One lady said I'd completely condemned her to Hell and was trying to make her jump through hoops. A few moments later another lady was telling me how helpful my words had been, and couldn't speak highly enough of me. Both had listened to the same sermon, but had come to very different conclusions. If I listened to what people said, and saw myself as they do, I would be so up and down I'd have a nervous breakdown every day! No. I am who God says I am. That is why I consider it most important to read his word every day. So he can sow the good seed of his word into my heart. So I am transformed by his word as it renews my mind.

"Do not conform any longer to the pattern of this world, but be transformed by the renewing of your mind. Then you will be able to test and approve what God's will is - his good, pleasing and perfect will." (Romans 12:2, NIV).

As we begin to declare God's word over people and situations, that seed we sow will reap a harvest. Every time I go to Rwanda I declare a blessing on that whole nation. I declare that war and genocide is over and the day of revival has come. I sow that word everywhere I go. It is not wishful thinking, it is seed sowing. God told Abraham that all nations would be blessed through him. Rwanda is included in 'all nations'. They shall be blessed by God, their provider and healer, in the name of Jesus. Numbers 23:19 says, *"God is not a man, that He should lie, Nor a son of man, that He should repent. Has He said, and will He not do? Or has He spoken, and will He not make it good?"*

Your thoughts are a seed. They will have a harvest. When our children were babies, we nursed them. They got bigger. Our elder daughter is now taller than I am. When she was born I could hold her in one hand. Now she is bigger than I am. If you are nursing a grudge, it's going to get bigger. One day it will become bigger than you. If you are nursing a grudge, stop it. Put it down and let it starve and die. Stop sowing your time and thoughts into it.

Someone once said, *"We are crucified between two things: regret for yesterday and fear of tomorrow."* When we worry and dwell on fear, we are allowing Satan to sow his lies into our heart. As we water them by our meditation and worry, we help them to grow. We will then begin speaking our faith in the devil's lies, thus sowing more seeds of fear and worry. Eventually we get the harvest we had feared. But when we choose to believe what God says, in spite of the circumstance, we sow the seeds of faith. We need to meditate on God's word, turn it over in our mind, learn it by heart, speak it to others and speak it out in our prayers. Then we will reap a harvest.

Gardening and farming are not for weaklings. It takes hard work and patience. You don't sow a seed one minute and collect the harvest an hour later. It takes time - days, weeks, sometimes months. If we are growing a tree, it may take years before the first harvest. Galatians 6:9 says, *"Let us not become weary in doing good, for at the proper time we will reap a harvest if we do not give up."*

If you have a vision and a call from God, you need to begin sowing into that vision. Let the vision occupy your thoughts and actions. Sow into it with words so that it may grow. Dream dreams and write them down. Some Christians don't plan for the future. They say they're are just trusting the Lord. Sure we should trust the Lord, but sometimes that's a cop out. The Bible says it's good to make plans.

"Plans fail for lack of counsel, but with many advisers they succeed." (Proverbs 15:22).

Many years ago I sowed my time, thoughts, words, energy and money into a vision. I have the harvest today, the vision has come into being. The birth was very painful. But now the baby vision is growing well. The vision is now developing and growing in new ways I didn't foresee, but all the growth complies with the original vision to preach the word of God, in all the world, by all means possible. The Bible says, *"Write the vision and make it plain on tablets, that he may run who reads it."* (Habakkuk 2:2). When we sow a vision from God with the seeds of our mouth, thoughts and actions, we will reap a harvest.

The Bible says that money is also a seed. The Bible has ten times more verses about money than about salvation or healing. But most us don't want to hear preachers speaking or writing about money. It's too sensitive a subject. Let us put our sensitivities to one side and look at a few things the Bible says about money.

When we sow money into God's kingdom, he will multiply it. *"Do not be deceived, God is not mocked; for whatever a man sows, that he will also reap."* (Galatians 6:7). *'Well, isn't that just talking about spiritual things?'* Well look what the Bible says in another place, written by the same person.

"Remember this: Whoever sows sparingly will also reap sparingly, and whoever sows generously will also reap generously. Each man should give what he has decided in his heart to give, not reluctantly or under compulsion, for God loves a cheerful giver. And God is able to make all grace abound to you, so that in all things at all times, having all that you need, you will abound in every good work. As it is written: "He has scattered abroad his gifts to the poor; his righteousness endures for ever." Now he who supplies seed to the sower and bread for food will also supply and increase your store of seed and will enlarge the harvest of your righteousness. You will be made rich in every way so that you can be generous on every occasion, and through us your generosity will result in thanksgiving to God. This service that you perform is not only supplying the needs of God's people but is also overflowing in many expressions of thanks to God." (2 Corinthians 9:6-12, NIV).

Now these verses talk clearly about sowing money and reaping money. *"You will be made rich in every way so that you can be generous on every occasion, and through us your generosity will result in thanksgiving to God."*

When he knows he can trust us with a little, he will give us more. Luke 16:10-12 says, *"Whoever can be trusted with very little can also be trusted with much, and whoever is dishonest with very little will also be dishonest with much. So if you have not been trustworthy in handling worldly wealth, who will trust you with true riches? And if you have not been trustworthy with someone else's property, who will give you property of your own?"*

However, it isn't really right to give under a cloud of guilt. *"Each man should give what he has decided in his heart to give, not reluctantly or under compulsion, for God loves a cheerful giver."* (2 Corinthians 9:7, NIV). It may be that if you are not familiar with generous giving you may need to work towards it, increasing your offerings each week until you are cheerful about what you are giving. But with the measure we use it will be measured back to us.

Our faith is also a seed. Jesus said, *"It is like a mustard seed, which a man took and put in his garden; and it grew and became a large tree, and the birds of the air nested in its branches."* (Luke 13:19). Faith may seem small but it can achieve incredible results. When we sow faith, we will produce a harvest. This book was written in faith. At the time of writing I couldn't see how it would be published. But I believed that God called me to write it, and the fact you are now reading it is the harvest of my faith back then. The Bible says, *"Now faith is being sure of what we hope for and certain of what we do not see."* (Hebrews 11:1).

Faith is focussed on Jesus. We must allow him to meet our needs in the way he sees fit. We can sow a seed of faith and believe God will intervene in a situation, but we must allow

Jesus to get all the glory through his answer. We can never imagine the wonderful ways that God has in mind to answer the prayer of faith.

"For my thoughts are not your thoughts, neither are your ways my ways," declares the Lord. "As the heavens are higher than the earth, so are my ways higher than your ways and my thoughts than your thoughts. As the rain and the snow come down from heaven, and do not return to it without watering the earth and making it bud and flourish, so that it yields seed for the sower and bread for the eater, so is my word that goes out from my mouth: It will not return to me empty, but will accomplish what I desire and achieve the purpose for which I sent it." (Isaiah 55:8-11).

Even the seed we sow is given by God, so he should get all the glory and praise for the miracle of sowing and reaping. I pray that God will give you good seed to sow in your life so you can begin to turn your life around, and see increased blessing in every area of your life. "Now *may He who supplies seed to the sower, and bread for food, supply and multiply the seed you have sown and increase the fruits of your righteousness,"* (2 Corinthians 9:10).

This truth of reaping what we sow not only affects every area of our life, but it will be true all the days of your life. God said, *"While the earth remains, Seedtime and harvest ... shall not cease."* (Genesis 8:22). What are you sowing in your life?

8. Stepping into the Promise

The book of Joshua is the handbook for breakthrough. If you are trying to get a breakthrough in your life, then you need to study and meditate on the book of Joshua. It is the account of how God's people came from the wilderness to a land flowing with milk and honey. From the place of 'just enough', to the place of 'more than enough.' The journey had begun in Egypt, a place of 'not enough.' That is the pattern for God's restoration of his people: *Not enough - Just enough - More than enough.* But the story also marks a turning point for Joshua personally. A turning point that many Christians are at today.

"After the death of Moses the servant of the Lord, it came to pass that the Lord spoke to Joshua the son of Nun, Moses' assistant, saying: "Moses My servant is dead. Now therefore, arise, go over this Jordan, you and all this people, to the land which I am giving to them - the children of Israel." (Joshua 1:1,2).

Now why did God say, *"Moses is dead"?* At the end of the previous book of the Bible we read, *"And the children of Israel wept for Moses in the plains of Moab thirty days. So the days of weeping and mourning for Moses ended."* (Deuteronomy 34:8).

They had been weeping for Moses' death for thirty days. It wasn't news that Moses was dead. So why did God say that to Joshua? Well, Joshua had been used to standing behind Moses. He was Moses' assistant. But now Moses was dead, it was up to Joshua to make the decisions. It was time for him to step from the shadows onto centre stage. An era had ended. The era of the wilderness and having just enough was over. The promised land was now in sight across the Jordan river. This is what they had been aiming at for forty years in the wilderness. Now it was time for Joshua to arise to the position of leadership God had been preparing him for. This was his day. The day of promise had arrived. It was within their grasp. But there were enemies in the land, so how could they step into the promise of God?

The first instruction from God was *'Arise'*. It was time to rise up and take what belonged to God's people. Today it is time for the Joshuas of this nation to arise and take from the enemy what belongs to the people of God. It is time to arise and stand for truth. It is time to arise and do warfare with the enemy. It is time to be strong and courageous. It is time to cross our Jordan and step into the promise of God.

Some people have seen the promised land as a picture of heaven which will only become ours in the *'sweet by and by'*. But there were enemies in this land. There are no enemies in heaven. So the promised land speaks of now, today. Today we can enter into the land of *'more than enough'*, a land and a place of promise which God has declared is ours. And we can learn from Joshua how to overthrow the enemy who would keep us from stepping into the promise.

"Be strong and of good courage, for to this people you shall divide as an inheritance the land which I swore to their fathers to give them. Only be strong and very courageous, that you may observe to do according to all the law which Moses My servant commanded you; do not turn from it to the right hand or to the left, that you may prosper wherever you go." (Joshua 1:6,7).

God's second command was to be strong and courageous. God says this to Joshua repeatedly. Why? Because Joshua was feeling weak and fearful. But there is a big difference between *feeling* frightened and *being* frightened. Everyone feels frightened sometimes. But they don't all let the fear control them. Many people *feel* frightened and then *become* frightened - they allow the fear to control them. And fear is a paralysing force when we allow it to take root in our life.

When Hazel and I left our home and our secure jobs to move

to London, so I could train for ministry, a man at church said, "But what happens if it doesn't work out?"

"Well," I said, "I expect we will come back here and start all over again. But I don't want to grow old and wonder, 'what if...'. I'd rather take a risk and see what happens." Faith is spelt R.I.S.K.

Robert Schuller said, *"I would rather attempt something great for God and fail, than attempt nothing for God and succeed."* We cannot move forward in the plans and purposes of God by sitting on our blessed assurance. We have to stand up and walk in the Spirit.

"This Book of the Law shall not depart from your mouth, but you shall meditate in it day and night, that you may observe to do according to all that is written in it. For then you will make your way prosperous, and then you will have good success." (Joshua 1:8).

The third thing God instructed Joshua to do was to focus on the word of God and not the problem. This is the real key to faith in action. Believe what God says, not what others say. Paul wrote to the Romans, *"Let God be true but every man a liar."* (Romans 3:4). That was the problem in the story of David and Goliath. All the soldiers were looking at the problem, instead of at God who is bigger than the problem. The soldiers looked at Goliath and said, "He's so big, how can we win?" But David looked at him and said, "He's so big, how can I miss?" The enemy of God's people will always try to intimidate us, to move us from faith to fear.

Every mission I have ever been involved in has produced a side issue that had power to distract attention and create fear, unless we fixed our minds on the word and purposes of God.

As Joshua and the people looked across the Jordan, they would have remembered a day many years before when some of them went into the promised land. In Numbers 13 we read of

Moses sending some men to spy out the land of Canaan. Among them were two men of faith, Joshua and Caleb. What happened that day is very sobering when we are trying to move in faith ourself. The men went to the same place, but their assessment of the situation differed.

"Then they told him, and said: "We went to the land where you sent us. It truly flows with milk and honey, and this is its fruit." (Numbers 13:27).

This bit they were all agreed on. It was a land flowing with milk and honey, and they even brought back some of the fruit to prove it. After eating manna every day for forty years this must have been a very exciting prospect. However, that is where the similarities in their assessment end. Some of the men went on,

"Nevertheless the people who dwell in the land are strong; the cities are fortified and very large; moreover we saw the descendants of Anak there." (Numbers 13:28).

Notice now that the focus has shifted from the promise of God, to the problem in taking it. The descendants of Anak were giants feared by all, just as Goliath was by the Israelites years later.

"Then Caleb quieted the people before Moses, and said, "Let us go up at once and take possession, for we are well able to overcome it." But the men who had gone up with him said, "We are not able to go up against the people, for they are stronger than we." And they gave the children of Israel a bad report of the land which they had spied out, saying, "The land through which we have gone as spies is a land that devours its inhabitants, and all the people whom we saw in it are men of great stature. There we saw the giants (the descendants of Anak came from the giants); and we were like grasshoppers in our own sight, and so we were in their sight." (Numbers 13:30-33).

Caleb looked at the fact that God had given them this land.

It was theirs to take by faith. But the other men began speaking out the fear and the problems. The more they spoke about it the more fearful they became. They began to see themselves as grasshoppers. If you think of yourself as an insect, you will begin acting like an insect. *"For as he thinks in his heart, so is he."* (Proverbs 23:7). Then God responded to this argument.

"Say to them, `As I live,' says the Lord, `just as you have spoken in My hearing, so I will do to you: `The carcasses of you who have complained against Me shall fall in this wilderness, all of you who were numbered, according to your entire number, from twenty years old and above. `Except for Caleb the son of Jephunneh and Joshua the son of Nun, you shall by no means enter the land which I swore I would make you dwell in." (Numbers 14:28-30).

Caleb and Joshua said they could take the land, because God said they could. The rest said they would be defeated, the enemies were too strong. *Everyone got what they said.* All the others died in the wilderness and never entered the promised land - *just as they said* - they were not able to enter it. Only Caleb and Joshua survived and entered the promised land and overcame the enemies, *just as they had said.* Joshua and Caleb operated in faith, the rest in fear. Everyone got what they said. Be careful what you say. Now, all these years later, Joshua was the one who sent spies into the land.

"Now Joshua the son of Nun sent out two men from Acacia Grove to spy secretly, saying, "Go, view the land, especially Jericho." So they went, and came to the house of a harlot named Rahab, and lodged there." (Joshua 2:1).

It is interesting that they ended up at Rahab's house. It is likely that Rahab kept an inn, and, as many did in those days, also worked as a prostitute. Rahab not only helped them to avoid capture, but she gave them some very important information.

"Now before they lay down, she came up to them on the

roof, and said to the men: "I know that the Lord has given you the land, that the terror of you has fallen on us, and that all the inhabitants of the land are fainthearted because of you. For we have heard how the Lord dried up the water of the Red Sea for you when you came out of Egypt, and what you did to the two kings of the Amorites who were on the other side of the Jordan, Sihon and Og, whom you utterly destroyed. And as soon as we heard these things, our hearts melted; neither did there remain any more courage in anyone because of you, for the Lord your God, He is God in heaven above and on earth beneath." (Joshua 2:8-11).

So, although the enemy and their fortress looked very powerful, it was actually a foregone conclusion that Israel would take the land. This was good news. It also tells us that, as far as Satan is concerned, it is a foregone conclusion that you will have the victory over him, because he has heard about the blood of Jesus shed on the cross for you. He is terrified of you because he knows that Jesus, the Anointed One and his Anointing, lives in you, the believer.

The story of Rahab also speaks of the goodness of God. Here was a woman who was not only on the enemy's side, but she was an immoral woman too. Yet when she heard about the people of Israel, she concluded, *"The Lord your God, He is God in heaven above and on earth beneath."* And there came about a covenant of protection for Rahab and her family because she helped God's people and acknowledged that God was God. The Bible says it was by her faith that she was rescued.

"By faith the harlot Rahab did not perish with those who did not believe, when she had received the spies with peace." (Hebrews 11:31).

And James commends Rahab for putting her faith into action. "Likewise, *was not Rahab the harlot also justified by works when she received the messengers and sent them out another way?"* (James 2:25).

The spies entered into a covenant agreement with Rahab based on a scarlet cord. She was to tie the scarlet cord in the window and then everyone in the house would be spared when Israel attacked Jericho.

"So the men said to her: "We will be blameless of this oath of yours which you have made us swear, unless, when we come into the land, you bind this line of scarlet cord in the window through which you let us down, and unless you bring your father, your mother, your brothers, and all your father's household to your own home. So it shall be that whoever goes outside the doors of your house into the street, his blood shall be on his own head, and we will be guiltless. And whoever is with you in the house, his blood shall be on our head if a hand is laid on him. And if you tell this business of ours, then we will be free from your oath which you made us swear." Then she said, "According to your words, so be it." And she sent them away, and they departed. And she bound the scarlet cord in the window." (Joshua 2:17-21).

This incident yet again foreshadows the blood of Jesus. The scarlet cord is like the blood of Christ which protects those who receive it from destruction. It also was the means of escape for the spies, their way of salvation from enemy forces. For Rahab and her family, the scarlet cord was like the blood of the Passover lamb on the door posts of the homes of Israel when they were in Egypt.

Joshua chapter three tells of how Israel crossed the Jordan into the promised land. Here we find more keys to our own breakthrough. *"Then Joshua rose early in the morning; and they set out from Acacia Grove and came to the Jordan, he and all the children of Israel, and lodged there before they crossed over."* (Joshua 3:1).

Joshua rose early in the morning. By nature I am not really

an early morning person. But if we are ever to get the break-throughs we are hoping for, we will have to get up in the morning and be with God. Prayer is the major key to breakthrough. There are so many ways to pray and meet with God. The important thing is to hear from God. Prayer is a two way conversation. Not just us reciting a shopping list of needs, though it may include some of that. One man said, "It suddenly dawned on me. Here am I, someone who knows nothing about anything, having a conversation with God who knows everything about everything, and I was doing all the talking!?"

"For thus says the Lord GOD, the Holy One of Israel: "In returning and rest you shall be saved; In quietness and confidence shall be your strength..." (Isaiah 30:15).

"Your ears shall hear a word behind you, saying, "This is the way, walk in it..." (Isaiah 30:21).

Before we take the land that God has given to us, we must hear from him about the strategy he has chosen for us to get the victory.

9. Taking the Land

Another thing Joshua used to enter into God's promise was faith. Faith that God had spoken and had given them the land they were about to possess. To see breakthrough in our life we need a word from God. And we need to mix faith with that word.

"For indeed the gospel was preached to us as well as to them; but the word which they heard did not profit them, not being mixed with faith in those who heard it." (Hebrews 4:2).

This is what all the heroes of faith did. They took God at his word and mixed faith with the word. They declared God's word as true in their life, and in due course they received the fruit of their faith. Abraham, the man of faith, is a good example.

"[Abraham] who, contrary to hope, in hope believed, so that he became the father of many nations, according to what was spoken, "So shall your descendants be." And not being weak in faith, he did not consider his own body, already dead (since he was about a hundred years old), and the deadness of Sarah's womb. He did not waver at the promise of God through unbelief, but was strengthened in faith, giving glory to God, and being fully convinced that what He had promised He was also able to perform. And therefore "it was accounted to him for righteousness." Now it was not written for his sake alone that it was imputed to him, but also for us. It shall be imputed to us who believe in Him who raised up Jesus our Lord from the dead" (Romans 4:18-24).

Joshua prayed in faith. He rose early, moved the people to the edge of the Jordan and they camped there that night. So much happened under Joshua's command before the people crossed the Jordan. Faith and patience go together. Many people fail to achieve their goal because they expect everything to be instant. They rush in where angels fear to tread. They don't seek wisdom before they act. Often it ends in tears. Lack of patience is often a sign of immaturity.

Now Joshua wasn't going to wait forever. He had heard God say *'within three days'*. But although he knew he had the land from God, he didn't make the mistake of rushing in and getting ahead of God. Patience will always be required when we begin to move in faith.

"But the ones that fell on the good ground are those who, having heard the word with a noble and good heart, keep it and bear fruit with patience." (Luke 8:15).

"By your patience possess your souls." (Luke 21:19). Too many people are praying 'Lord give me patience. But do it quickly!'

Then in Joshua 3:3 the people are told to follow the ark of the covenant across the Jordan. As we move in faith for a breakthrough, we must understand that we are a covenant people. We must have the blood of Jesus as the basis for our breakthrough. We must have the word that God has spoken about our situation, on our lips. We must follow the covenant principles.

Abraham lost patience when waiting for his promised son of blessing. He tried to help God out by sleeping with the slave woman. And so, Ishmael was born. But he was not the child of promise, and actually caused more problems. So we need to stand on what God has said and be patient for God to bring it about. We must be careful not to force an Ishmael, but wait for an Isaac.

Joshua 3:4 says that they should make sure they could see the ark of the covenant carried before them, *"...that you may know the way by which you must go, for you have not passed this way before."* As we learn about faith that gets a breakthrough, we have to learn from God because we *'have not passed this way before.'* The writer to the Hebrews put it this way, *"Let us fix our eyes on Jesus, the author and perfecter of our faith..."* (Hebrews 12:2, NIV). There is also peace in learning from Jesus, how to walk in the Spirit. Jesus said, *"...learn from Me... and you will find rest for your souls."* (Matthew 11:29).

The rest of Joshua 3 tells how the Jordan parted so the people went through on dry land. Here God confirms what he had said to Joshua, *"This day I will begin to exalt you in the sight of all Israel, that they may know that, as I was with Moses, so I will be with you."* (Joshua 3:7).

In Joshua 5 there is a time of restoring holiness. The act of circumcision had long been abandoned. Now it was restored. Humanly speaking, it was the worst time to reinstate this practice. Imagine all the armed forces of Israel limping delicately towards Jericho trying to look intimidating, yet trying to avoid sudden movement in the groin area!

"So it was, when they had finished circumcising all the people, that they stayed in their places in the camp till they were healed. Then the LORD said to Joshua, "This day I have rolled away the reproach of Egypt from you." Therefore the name of the place is called Gilgal to this day. Now the children of Israel camped in Gilgal, and kept the Passover on the fourteenth day of the month at twilight on the plains of Jericho." (Joshua 5:8-10).

The Passover, also, had long been abandoned. It was only kept for one year after leaving Egypt. Now it was restored. As the children of God step into the promises of God, righteousness will be restored. Lifestyles will come into line with God's word.

Joshua and the people of Israel were moving closer to taking Jericho, the first stronghold - the key to the rest of the promised land. However, more changes were yet to happen.

"Then the manna ceased on the day after they had eaten the produce of the land; and the children of Israel no longer had manna, but they ate the food of the land of Canaan that year." (Joshua 5:12).

For the best part of 40 years, Israel had eaten manna in the desert. Manna - the supernatural provision of God - just enough for each day. Manna was a welcome miracle in the desert . When there was a time of 'not enough' it was good to move into 'just enough'.

"...he who gathered much did not have too much, and he who gathered little did not have too little. Each one gathered as much as he needed." (Exodus 16:18, NIV).

However, manna was the same, day in and day out. It was just enough, but after 40 years, perhaps a little boring. It was a short term fix, not God's long term best. So it was that as they entered into the promise, the manna ceased and they ate the beautiful fruits of the promised land. If we are to step into the promise we must embrace change. Joshua, too, was about to face a massive change in his understanding.

"And it came to pass, when Joshua was by Jericho, that he lifted his eyes and looked, and behold, a Man stood opposite him with His sword drawn in His hand. And Joshua went to Him and said to Him, "Are You for us or for our adversaries?" So He said, "No, but as Commander of the army of the LORD I have now come." And Joshua fell on his face to the earth and worshipped, and said to Him, "What does my Lord say to His servant?" Then the Commander of the LORD'S army said to Joshua, "Take your sandal off your foot, for the place where you stand is holy." And Joshua did so." (Joshua 5:13-15).

Joshua saw a stranger standing with a drawn sword, and asked him, *"Are You for us or for our adversaries?"* But the stranger said, *"No."* A strange answer to the question. It is also a strange answer in the Middle East, where everyone is on someone's side and the divisions are very clear. Are you for Jews or Arabs, Christians or Muslims, Protestants or Catholics? But the stranger said, *"No, but as Commander of the army of the LORD I have now come."* God had not come to take sides, but to take over.

Joshua, as an experienced army commander, no doubt had the strategy for taking Jericho all sorted out. God now turned up, took over and ordered a *March for Jehovah,* with the ram's horn trumpet, or Hebrew shophar, as the principal weapon.

The main key for breakthrough is obedience to God, even when you think your plan was more sensible. It was Joshua's willingness to humble himself under God, take off his shoes and bow with his face to the ground, to announce the seven day praise march and carry it out, that won the victory of Jericho, and subsequently opened up the rest of the promised land to Israel.

"Now Jericho was securely shut up because of the children of Israel; none went out, and none came in. And the LORD said to Joshua: "See! I have given Jericho into your hand, its king, and the mighty men of valour." (Joshua 6:1,2).

'Now Jericho was securely shut up because of the children of Israel'. As we obey God and move in faith, Satan has to shut up. He cannot stand the resistance fighters of heaven - you and me - moving in faith, obedience and holiness.

"Therefore submit to God. Resist the devil and he will flee from you." (James 4:7).

Notice the order there. First, submit to God. Second resist the devil. Third, he will flee from you. Satan knows that our victory is a foregone conclusion. His only weapons are lies and intimidation. When he lies, he speaks his native language. Like a playground bully, he intimidates everyone and yet is filled with insecurities and self-doubt. He makes himself look the most powerful, when actually he is powerless against truth, faith and obedience to God. He sees the scarlet cord tied in the window of our heart and knows we are covenant people, numbered among the children of the Living God. He reminds us of our past, yet flees if we mention his future. As we move in faith, Satan has to shut up.

'And the LORD said to Joshua: "See! I have given Jericho into your hand, its king, and the mighty men of valour."' (Joshua 6:2).

The victory of breakthrough is won in the Spirit first, and then the natural world lines up with it. In 1989, I watched in amazement as the Berlin Wall was opened, and thousands of people climbed onto it and began to demolish the wall that had kept them imprisoned since 1961. How did it happen? The battle was won in the Spirit through prayer and spiritual warfare, first. Then the natural world lined up with the victory won in prayer. Among many others, Brother Andrew and Open Doors had been active in 'Seven Years of Prayer for the Soviet Union' prior to the wall coming down.

"For we do not wrestle against flesh and blood, but against principalities, against powers, against the rulers of the darkness of this age, against spiritual hosts of wickedness in the heavenly places." (Ephesians 6:12).

Our Berlin Walls and our Jerichos will fall, as we move in obedience and intimate fellowship with Jesus and his word.

So Jericho was taken and after it many other cities and kingdoms. At Ai in Joshua 7 they were reminded of the importance of integrity as Achan was put to death for stealing from the work of God. At the end of chapter 11 we read an interesting statement - another key to breakthrough.

"So Joshua took the whole land, according to all that the LORD had said to Moses; and Joshua gave it as an inheritance to Israel according to their divisions by their tribes. Then the land rested from war." (Joshua 11:23).

Joshua got all that God had promised him. But the telling phrase here is the final one. *'Then the land rested from war.'* To get any breakthrough in the kingdom is warfare. Satan does not give up ground without a fight. This is why many settle for second best. The price seems too high to step into our destiny. But we will never be the people we are meant to be, unless we pay the price and break through. Eleven chapters of war within and without, but the breakthrough came, and with it peace and prosperity. Certainly there were more wars to fight, but peace was established on the ground that had been taken. This is why we have to feed and nurture our fellowship with Jesus through Bible reading, prayer, meditation on the word, dreaming, planing and taking risks. We are here to enforce the victory that Jesus won on the cross, until he returns and fully establishes his reign of peace on the earth.

God has called you to be an overcomer. Even if your natural demeanour is quiet and a bit timid, God has given you power to overcome.

"You are of God, little children, and have overcome them, because He who is in you is greater than he who is in the world." (1 John 4:4). *"For whatever is born of God overcomes the world. And this is the victory that has overcome the world—our faith."* (1 John 5:4).

"For God did not give us a spirit of timidity, but a spirit of power, of love and of self-discipline." (2 Timothy 1:7, NIV).

It is time for the spirit of Joshua to rise up in you, to overcome the enemy, to take possession of your promised land. To stand in your destiny. To manifest the victory Jesus has already won for you. God says you are an overcomer. Listen to what he says you are. *Let God be true and every man a liar.* (Romans 3:4).

10. "Do I need sandwiches?"

The little boy who gave up his fish sandwiches that day, couldn't believe that Jesus could feed over 5,000 people with them. But in the hands of Jesus, even the most insignificant things, and people, can be blessed and broken and multiplied to feed a multitude.

In 1993, we were in the middle of a big town-wide campaign, telling people the good news of Jesus Christ. My friend, Kerry Dixon, asked if I could help him with a city-wide mission where thousands of people would attend each night. I sounded interested. Then he told me it was in the Philippines. He had been trying to get me to go there for some time, but the Philippines was all my fears rolled into one. I was very fussy about food, scared of insects, didn't like being too hot and didn't like being too far away from home, not to mention that I lacked the finance to go. I said I would *"pray about it"*.

As I prayed to God, I asked if it was OK with him if I didn't go. I felt God saying, "Is this it then? East Anglia? Is that as dangerous as the preaching of the gospel gets for you?"

Thinking about those who were missionaries living in far away places and those who had even died for their faith, I felt a bit silly. But God knew that, for me, going to the Philippines would need a deep miracle beyond anything I had seen before. I knew that I would speak to crowds much bigger than I was used to, and my faith might seem shallow in comparison to theirs. The furthest place I had ever travelled to was Dublin. That had been quite a culture shock.

I told Kerry that if God provided for the costs of the trip, I would go, and I would take God's provision as the sign of being called to this trip. Secretly, in my heart, I knew I wouldn't have to go because no one had ever given me £1,000 for ministry before. Why would they do so now? However, God has a

95

sense of humour. Kerry had asked me in September. By November, I was booked on a flight to the Philippines with Kerry, and Wendy Diaper, another 'victim' of the call to the Philippines. The money had all come in. O dear. How sad. Never mind.

The 13-hour flight was punctuated by drinks, food, entertainment, and well-groomed staff who couldn't do enough for us. For a few moments the trip seemed glamorous. Unfortunately, all this opulence was the worst possible preparation for what I was about to encounter. All the luxury of the airline was left behind on the aircraft as we entered the Third-World poverty of Manila International Airport. Everything seemed 30 years out of date, mainly because it was. And whereas the cabin crew had made our comfort their aim, the customs and airport staff seemed to make thwarting our progress their number one aim.

We eventually ran the gauntlet of taxi operators and money changers and negotiated a taxi to the domestic airport. Manila traffic is an every-man-for-himself experience. Broken-down vehicles, many without lights, charged through the Asian night as if they were in a demolition derby. Amazingly, we arrived safely at the domestic airport only to find that were we locked out overnight. So, we took our place sitting on the pavement and watched the world, several lizards, and a rather large cockroach go by.

I had thought Manila airport was a bit basic until we descended into Iloilo City airport on Panay Island - a single runway strip bordered by bamboo shanty houses on both sides. As we stepped from the plane at 5am, we discovered members of the church were waiting for us. They suddenly burst into song, unfurled a welcome banner and put garlands of flowers round our necks. I had never encountered a welcome like it.

Moments later, we were unloading the car at the home of the pastor who had invited us. His home was a small plywood house in a rural area. I was just getting my bag out of the car when I looked across a field, distorted by the heat haze of the early morning sun. As the strange sound of crickets filled the air, the presence of God came upon me. It was an incredible experience, as though God was saying, *"I will be with you always, even to the ends of the earth."* Surely, for this untravelled Englishman, this was the ends of the earth.

That night, as darkness fell over the city, I was taken to a shanty town where I was to speak at an open-air meeting. As the musicians began the first song, a rat skipped over my feet chased by a flea-bitten cat. The rat jumped over the guitar cases on the ground and disappeared into the darkness. I was called to preach. It was the first time I had spoken through an interpreter into an unknown culture, to a people I did not really understand. As I closed the message, the skies opened and torrential rain poured down on us. The trip was one adventure after another and I certainly learned more than I taught.

Were my fears realised? Yes. We did eat strange things such as worms and cats. The insects were large and in abundance. En suite rats and hot and cold running cockroaches were the order of the day. When it went dark, and I was in bed, with my mosquito net hermetically sealed to the mattress, I heard the gecko. A sort of cuckoo-sound announced the arrival of this lizard in the shadows of the bedroom. Geckos are about 2 feet long, but somehow, in the dark, I imagined something the size of a Labrador walking about in the room. Yes, my fears were realised, but I think the lesson was - *face the fear and do it anyway.*

But the people! The people were incredible. I visited many shanty towns. One was built over the beach, connected by a series of bamboo bridges, built to carry malnourished Filipinos, but which sometimes gave way under the weight of large and heavy Westerners. It was such a privilege to visit the homes of people who were living as a family of seven people, in what amounted to less than a garden shed. To see their love of Jesus, and hear them tell of his grace and mercy in their lives was a privilege. It was in those shanty towns that I really began to understand what an evil curse poverty is.

Kerry and Wendy left to visit another island while I stayed in Iloilo for the week, to speak at a pastors' conference and a crusade . I saw God heal many people and many became Christians. Sometimes when I stood up to preach, tears came instead of words. I still felt very inadequate but the power of God was at work.

Some days I found the limit of my tolerance, when it was pigs' intestine soup for lunch. I rearranged it in the dish but couldn't bring myself to eat it or dip my cat sandwich into it. Feeling immoderately peckish, I went for a walk in the city and began to hunt for somewhere to eat. I found a haven of Western civilisation called Dunkin Doughnuts. Smiling at the security guard on the door, who was holding an automatic rifle, I stepped into more familiar surroundings. The added bonus of this establishment was air-conditioning which, in the tropical heat of the Philippines, was very refreshing. After consuming an immodest amount of doughnuts and iced coke, I emerged back into the heat, with a light head and heavy everything else.

A week later, I joined Kerry and Wendy on the Island of Mindanao. I stayed at the 5,000-strong Happy Church. We were taken, one afternoon, to a jungle area where 300 people came to listen to the gospel. Over 120 people responded and received Christ into their heart. Some people brought a blind man to us. "You said Jesus healed people. Please heal this blind man."

We looked at each other and saw the opposite of faith in our faces. We laid hands on the man and prayed. "I can see light and dark." he said. We prayed again.

"I can see people but I can't see their faces." he said. We prayed again.

"I can see." he said, and he walked away into the crowd.

Two years later, I was back in the Philippines and met the pastor of the Happy Church. She told me that she had visited that area recently and met the man who had been blind. He could still see perfectly, and all those who became Christians that day were still in the church there.

After 3 weeks of intense tropical heat, the daily side effects of antimalarial drugs, and the stress of being immersed in a strange culture, I felt completely exhausted. I climbed aboard the plane to come home feeling like a shipwreck victim being winched to unexpected safety. Yet from the obedience of going on that trip, whole areas of new ministry and opportunities have sprung up. Fear and feeling inadequate can cripple us inside. But the perfect love of Jesus casts out all fear and sets us free.

When I was first invited to go to the Philippines, I was so ignorant about world travel. When I saw the flight would take 13 hours, I phoned Kerry to ask if I should bring sandwiches? He couldn't answer me for laughing. He still laughs about it today.

There was a little boy in the Bible who took some sandwiches on his journey and a strange thing happened to them. Jesus had been preaching in the middle of nowhere when he realised the people were getting hungry. It was going dark and it was miles to the nearest shop. Then Andrew found the little boy.

"There is a lad here who has five barley loaves and two small fish, but what are they among so many?" (John 6:9).

When people looked at what the boy had and then looked at the 5,000 people sitting there, it seemed obvious that the boy did not have enough to feed everybody. He didn't have what it takes. But he put what little he had into the hands of Jesus and miraculously it fed a multitude. They even collected the leftovers which filled twelve baskets.

We may feel inadequate as we face up to what God is calling us to do. We may be full of fear and our best efforts may seem futile. But when we put ourselves in the hands of Jesus, and allow him to bless us and break us, we can find ourselves feeding a multitude, going to the ends of the earth, and seeing a blind man healed.

You may feel inadequate to face certain things in your life. Today, put yourself unreservedly into the hands of Jesus, face your fears, allow him to bless you and break you. He will use you to feed a multitude. He will do it in such a way that there will even be a surplus when the miracle is finished.

In relationship with Jesus, even the most insignificant person becomes a powerful force for good. In relationship with Jesus, normal capacities or restrictions do not apply. In relationship with Jesus, you can make a difference to the world.

11. Rest for your Soul

I sense that Christians today are under pressure. For several years now, I have seen various Christian leaders, both lay people and clergy, under great pressure in their private lives. They may be battling with sickness in the family, broken relationships, trouble in the church fellowship, finances or other things. The backdrop to their personal situation has been the increase of social and spiritual darkness in society.

Others have looked to a Christian leader as their guide and inspiration, only to see that person fall from grace, through some lack of integrity or personal morality. The person they built their faith on has crumbled, leaving their hope and peace in shreds. Some have lost faith. Some hang in there by the skin of their teeth. In Matthew's gospel, Jesus gives us the strategy for holding on to our peace regardless of the circumstances.

"Come to Me, all you who labour and are heavy laden, and I will give you rest. Take My yoke upon you and learn from Me, for I am gentle and lowly in heart, and you will find rest for your souls. For My yoke is easy and My burden is light." (Matthew 11:28-30).

In these few verses, we find the wisdom of God for every breakthrough we desire and the method of keeping our peace - the peace that Jesus has given us. The main point of this teaching of Jesus is: "Learn *from me and you will find rest for your souls"*.

By letting Jesus teach us how to face each situation, his wisdom will bring peace to our soul. The soul is the mind, the will, and the emotions. It is the place where we can become exhausted after struggling with the troubles of life. This teaching of Jesus is perhaps best illustrated in the life of the prophet Elijah.

Elijah was destined to face the prophets of Baal on Mount Carmel and prove once and for all that the Living God is the

True God. But Elijah did not fall out of bed one morning and challenge the prophets of Baal. He learnt from God, little by little, so that when the big day came, his confidence in God was sure and steady.

Elijah is a good example because the Bible says, *"Elijah was a man just like us."* (James 5:17, NIV). Elijah began learning about God's power in small ways. In the days approaching the contest on Mount Carmel, we can see God teaching his servant the principles of faith.

Firstly, Elijah had a private miracle. God said he would command the birds to feed Elijah. In this first step of faith, there are no other witnesses. If it all went horribly wrong, no one else would know. It would be here, privately, in a close friendship with God, that Elijah would lay the foundation for the later miracles.

"Then the word of the LORD came to him, saying, "Get away from here and turn eastward, and hide by the Brook Cherith, which flows into the Jordan. And it will be that you shall drink from the brook, and I have commanded the ravens to feed you there." So he went and did according to the word of the LORD, for he went and stayed by the Brook Cherith, which flows into the Jordan. The ravens brought him bread and meat in the morning, and bread and meat in the evening; and he drank from the brook." (1 Kings 17:2-6).

Elijah watched the miracle of the birds feeding him everyday, and as he did so his faith in God, and his understanding of miracles, grew. Eventually, God moved him on to see a similar miracle of provision, but this time there would be a couple of witnesses.

"Then the word of the LORD came to him, saying, "Arise, go to Zarephath, which belongs to Sidon, and dwell there. See, I have commanded a widow there to provide for you."" (1 Kings 17:8-9).

He obeyed God and met the widow. Now, God said he had commanded the widow to provide for him. She was the one through whom his provision would come. But she didn't know it herself. So, when he met her, the circumstances contradicted what God had said. The widow was really despairing and was almost ready to die of starvation. How could she be the one who would provide for him? Had God got it wrong? Or had Elijah misunderstood?

"So she said, "As the LORD your God lives, I do not have bread, only a handful of flour in a bin, and a little oil in a jar; and see, I am gathering a couple of sticks that I may go in and prepare it for myself and my son, that we may eat it, and die." (1 Kings 17:12).

This did not look like God's abundant provision. But Elijah was learning from God, so he had rest in his soul. Then he spoke to the woman, not according to the circumstances, but according to faith in God's word. He enacted the first principle of faith. He declared something that was not, as though it was. This is how God created the world. It is the way Jesus healed the sick, fed multitudes and stilled storms. *"God...calls those things which do not exist as though they did;"* (Romans 4:17).

So Elijah declared what was going to happen in faith. *"And Elijah said to her, "Do not fear; go and do as you have said, but make me a small cake from it first, and bring it to me; and afterward make some for yourself and your son. For thus says the LORD God of Israel: `The bin of flour shall not be used up, nor shall the jar of oil run dry, until the day the LORD sends rain on the earth.'"* (1 Kings 17:13,14).

For the second time, Elijah watched the miracle unfold before his eyes just as he had spoken it into being, according to God's word. Then a greater test came to his faith. The widow's son died. Raising the dead was different to believing for the multiplication of food. But Elijah was in God's school of faith.

For this miracle of raising the dead there were just two witnesses again. Notice that Elijah did not focus his prayer on the problem but on the solution. He said what he desired.

"And he stretched himself out on the child three times, and cried out to the LORD and said, "O LORD my God, I pray, let this child's soul come back to him." Then the LORD heard the voice of Elijah; and the soul of the child came back to him, and he revived." (1 Kings 17:21-22).

Now he saw that God had the power to restore life to the dead. Not just in theory but before his very eyes. Here was another stepping stone towards the great test of faith that was to come on Mount Carmel. Elijah was living in a nation that was spiritually very dark. But as a result of his faith in action, at least one person was getting a revelation of the truth.

"Then the woman said to Elijah, "Now by this I know that you are a man of God, and that the word of the LORD in your mouth is the truth." (1 Kings 17:24).

The national contest for what was the truth was soon to come. But for now, the God of Elijah had won one of the local competitions.

Even after this victory, Mount Carmel wasn't rushed into. There is a very telling phrase at the beginning of the account of the contest on Mount Carmel. *"And it came to pass after many days..."* (1 Kings 18:1). During those many days, I suspect that Elijah still studied at the school of faith. He did what Jesus later said, '*Learn from me... and you will find rest for your souls.*'

In all the accounts of incredible miracles there is always something at stake. In creation - the very existence of mankind. In the crossing of the Red Sea - the word of God and the deliverance of his people Israel. In the manna in the wilderness - their survival. In the walls of Jericho falling down - the sovereignty of God. And so on. So it was on Mount Carmel. The honour and truth of God were at stake. One reason that we do not see as many miracles as we would like may be because we never take risks and put anything at stake. If God didn't show up on Mount Carmel, Elijah would lose the battle for truth, and very likely his own life.

Baal worship was a terrible thing. It was a pornographic religion whose temples were filled with images of sexual organs. Sexual perversion of every kind imaginable, and some that are not, were practised. Children were ritually abused and burned as a sacrifice to Baal. The child was laid on the altar and seemed to spontaneously burst into flames as the priests prayed. Archaeologists have discovered some temples of Baal and found a tunnel running underneath the temple to just under the altar. Traces of burning were found at the end of the tunnel. Evidence suggests that the priests of Baal used to tie up a child for sacrifice, and then someone would crawl through the tunnel and light a fire under the altar at the appropriate time to give the impression that Baal had consumed the child by fire. I don't know if Elijah knew this or if God revealed it to him, but to have the contest up a mountain was real wisdom. Here there could be no fixing of the result. Elijah was determined to bring the nation back to God.

"And Elijah came to all the people, and said, "How long will you falter between two opinions? If the LORD is God, follow Him; but if Baal, follow him." But the people answered him not a word." (1 Kings 18:21).

He arranged two altars on Carmel and challenged the prophets of Baal to a contest to decide who was the real God.

"Then you call on the name of your gods, and I will call on the name of the LORD; and the God who answers by fire, He is God." So all the people answered and said, "It is well spoken." (1 Kings 18:24).

He let them go first and ridiculed them as they called out day and night to Baal.

"At noon Elijah began to taunt them. "Shout louder!" he said. "Surely he is a god! Perhaps he is deep in thought, or busy, or travelling. Maybe he is sleeping and must be awakened." (1 Kings 18:27, NIV).

By comparison, Elijah prayed only a short prayer, but one full of faith, and the fire came down. The argument about who was the true God was settled once and for all. The miracle sent shock waves through the nation and a death threat was issued to Elijah. So often, it is immediately after we have our greatest victory in the Spirit that the devil attacks and seems to bring everything into turmoil. What a victory Elijah had just witnessed but now he had lost his peace and began working from fear, the opposite of faith.

"...he arose and ran for his life, and went to Beersheba, which belongs to Judah, and left his servant there. But he himself went a day's journey into the wilderness, and came and sat down under a broom tree. And he prayed that he might die, and said, "It is enough! Now, LORD, take my life, for I am no better than my fathers!" (1 Kings 19:3,4).

Elijah was exhausted both physically and emotionally. But God had a plan to restore him to health and peace.

Firstly, he slept. The angel woke him up and fed him and then he slept again. (1 Kings 19:5-7). Sleep is healing. That's why hospitals are always full of beds! If you're exhausted, get some sleep. Some people feel guilty about sleeping and resting. But sleep is a gift from God. *"He makes me to lie down... He leads me beside the still waters."* (Psalms 23:2). In the book of Esther, Mordeciah and all the Israelites are rescued from execution... *as they sleep.* (Esther 6).

Secondly, Elijah found the voice of God. *"Then [God] said, "Go out, and stand on the mountain before the LORD." And behold, the LORD passed by, and a great and strong wind tore into the mountains and broke the rocks in pieces before the*

LORD, but the LORD was not in the wind; and after the wind an earthquake, but the LORD was not in the earthquake; and after the earthquake a fire, but the LORD was not in the fire; and after the fire a still small voice." (1 Kings 19:11-12).

Elijah was brought to stillness and quietness and then he heard God's voice. If we are to be used by God, we must develop a quietness and stillness to hear the still small voice of God. One translation calls this *'a thin silence'*. God is not going to shout. He expects us to make some quietness so that we may hear the still small voice, the thin silence, the gentle whisper of his voice. The Bible says, *"In returning and rest you shall be saved; In quietness and confidence shall be your strength."* (Isaiah 30:15).

Thirdly, he brought him into partnership with Elisha. (1 Kings 19:19-21). There is something powerful about partnership. *"As iron sharpens iron, So a man sharpens the countenance of his friend."* (Proverbs 27:17). I have been very blessed over the years by the people that God has brought me into partnership with. Some friendships are ones that help me relax. Others are ministry relationships and friendships with mentors. I would say that my favourite and most rewarding relationship is the one I have with my wife, Hazel. I'm not saying that because it's the Christian thing to say, but because it is true. Like all marriages, we have our ups and downs, but as we have grown in our commitment to each other over the years, our relationship is a refreshing and rewarding one. This, along with other relationships of refreshment and restoration, keeps my spiritual life fresh and healthy. Elisha gave Elijah a second wind. And he was a blessing to him. He was a man of radical vision and when it came time for Elijah to leave this world, he asked Elisha what he wanted. True to character he said, *'I'll have twice the anointing you have.'* And he received too.

Sleep, the word of God and partnership are God's strategy

for restoring the weary. If you're tired and weary, it is time to learn from Jesus, to hear the still small voice, to come into God-ordained relationships. Jesus says to you, *"Learn from me and you will find rest for your souls"*.

12. Valley of Dry Bones

The army jeep bumped along the mountain road in Kibungu district in Rwanda. The armed guard, sitting precariously on the back of the jeep, somehow managed to stay onboard. I wasn't exactly sure where we were going. Eventually, after many hours of bumpy roads, we arrived at a Catholic church. Much of the village had been levelled in the genocide of 1994. The school gates were padlocked. The priest was sent for and came with the key. He looked very tired and weary. He unlocked the gates and the soldiers waved their guns, signalling me to go in.

I had visited many African schools before this one. They were always alive with the sound of children talking, laughing and singing. But here, there was silence. Strangely, there was no bird song.

As I approached the first classroom, a vision of hell greeted my eyes. There, in every classroom, lay hundreds of dead bodies. Most had become skeletons, yet still wore the clothes they were wearing on the day of the massacre in 1994. Some lay decapitated. Death filled the air. Smashed skulls of children lay next to the bones of their parents.

I began to understand more of the pain I had seen in the eyes of the people. The feeling of defeat which permeated the national thinking. I realised that this was not a tribal problem. Nor a political problem. This was a spiritual problem. It began the day Cain killed Abel in Genesis 4. God found Cain and said, *"What have you done? The voice of your brother's blood cries out to Me from the ground."* (Genesis 4:10).

Of course, any murder is devastating, but God uses this strange phrase, *"The voice of your brother's blood cries out to Me from the ground."* It sounds as if the blood of one murdered man disturbed the spiritual realms enough for God to hear. What does this tell us about the spiritual state of the nation of Rwanda where over one million people were massacred. The nation is sick. The land needs the healing of God.

In Europe, the blood of 20,000,000 men cries out from the battlefields of France in the 20th century alone. In Germany, the blood of 6,000,000 Jews cries out to God from the ground. We live in a sick and disturbed world. A world full of dry bones.

God has answered this bloodshed by the shedding of the blood of Jesus. But whereas human bloodshed causes disturbance, the shedding of Christ's blood brings peace. The Bible says, *"For it pleased the Father ...by Him to reconcile all things to Himself, ... having made peace through the blood of His cross."* (Colossians 1:19-20). The Bible says we have come to *"Jesus the Mediator of the new covenant, and to the blood of sprinkling that speaks better things than that of Abel."* (Hebrews 12:24).

What happened in Rwanda was diabolical. It was demonic. The terrible things done to people before and after they died, did not have their origin in a human mind. This thing came from the devil himself. Jesus said, *"The thief does not come except to steal, and to kill, and to destroy."* (John 10:10). The devil had been given free reign. He had used ordinary people, brainwashed by hatred and fear, to steal and to kill, and to destroy. To this day, the bones of many of those who were slaughtered in Rwanda lie where they fell in 1994. I have since returned to Rwanda on many occasions, and every time I visit a new area, I am shown another church where the bodies of thousands of men, women and children still lie today.

In the spiritual valleys of every nation, dry bones lie on the ground longing for a word of hope. Dry bones of people who are not dead physically, but spiritually they are dry bones. Ezekiel had a vision of a valley of dry bones.

"The hand of the Lord came upon me and brought me out in the Spirit of the Lord, and set me down in the midst of the val-

ley; and it was full of bones. Then He caused me to pass by them all around, and behold, there were very many in the open valley; and indeed they were very dry. And He said to me, "Son of man, can these bones live?" So I answered, "O Lord God, You know."

Again He said to me, "Prophesy to these bones, and say to them, `O dry bones, hear the word of the Lord! 'Thus says the Lord God to these bones: "Surely I will cause breath to enter into you, and you shall live. I will put sinews on you and bring flesh upon you, cover you with skin and put breath in you; and you shall live. Then you shall know that I am the Lord." (Ezekiel 37:1-6).

We see in Ezekiel's vision the very nature of God. He is the God who creates, the God who restores, the God who makes all things new. So often the Church, which should have been bringing the message of hope, has been like that valley of dry bones. A shadow of what God wanted it to be. In some places you may find only the dead bones of religion, instead of a living, vibrant community of believers. In our day, God is calling his people to speak his word to dry bones. As Ezekiel spoke God's word to the bones, they came to life, were clothed with flesh, and formed a mighty army. That is God's plan for his church. The days of going through the motions of religion are over.

It is the end of the road for hypocrisy. Time has run out for those playing at church. It is the end of the season for dead religion. The wind of the Spirit is blowing away the cobwebs and dust of dead tradition. History keepers will be replaced by history makers. The light of Jesus Christ is shining on the church of our day. He will expose everything of darkness and unholiness in his church, because he is making all things new. The middle ground is disappearing. The darkness around us is getting darker. But God's light and power are being released in a massive increase of his miracles in the world. The days of grey are giving way to days of black and white, good and evil. Many corrupt, compromised and apostate church bureaucracies will fall in the next decade. More dead churches will close down. Those preaching the uncompromised word of God will enter a period of abundant provision for the spreading of the gospel across the nations.

God told Ezekiel to speak God's word to the bones. *"I will cause breath to enter into you, and you shall live."* The breath of the Holy Spirit is blowing through the church. Never again must we make a monument out of a movement of God. People are being healed. Debts are being cancelled. In some places, the dead are being raised up to life.

Even in Rwanda, where the church has suffered a massive blow from Satan, God is restoring his people. In one of our meetings, we were praying for the sick. A lady had been listening to me preach at several meetings. She came forward and said, *"I have been listening to this man during these days. But I didn't know he was a Mzungu* (a white man) *because I was blind. But as you were praying, I began to see his white face. When I looked around, I realised I could see!"*

Another lady had very poor eyesight - even with glasses she could not see the words on the page of a book. Now she said she had been healed. Another lady had been in great pain in her abdomen, but now that pain had gone. And so the testimonies went on.

The Russian revolution was brought about by only 1% of the population. They didn't need a majority, just committed people. They overthrew the status quo and changed history. They didn't change things for the better because they left Jesus out of the equation. Revolution means to turn round. That's what usually happens in a revolution. One group of sinners is turned out and replaced by another group of sinners. Revolutions can change everything except what really matters - they cannot change the human heart. Che Guevara once said, *"If our revolution is not aimed at changing people, then I am not interested."*

Ezekiel had another word from God. God promised to change the hearts of the people. God says, *"I will give you a new heart and put a new spirit within you; I will take the heart of stone out of your flesh and give you a heart of flesh."* (Ezekiel 36:26). God wants to exchange a hard sinful heart for a sensitive heart of flesh. A heart that feels what he feels and desires what he desires. This is what begins to happen when we receive Jesus Christ into our heart.

If you and I rise up in obedience to the word of God in Christ Jesus, we will make a difference. If we become true disciples of Jesus we will make an impact on the world. The late David Watson wrote, *"Christians in the West have largely neglected what it means to be a disciple of Christ. The vast majority of western Christians are church members, pew fillers, hymn singers, sermon tasters, Bible readers, even born-again believers or Spirit-filled charismatics, but not true disciples of Jesus."*

God is speaking to his people. He is speaking to those who are very dry. He is telling you that he will, *"put breath in you; and you shall live."* The Hebrew word for breath is *'ruwach'*, the same word as for *'spirit'*. He will put his Spirit in you and you shall live.

Every time I return to Rwanda, I can see how God has brought new hope and new life to that nation. I am praying that this will continue and increase. However, the whole church across the world is hearing the word of God as never before. He is speaking to the dry bones of the Church and calling her from slumber. You and I have a part to play. We need to stand up and allow God to clothe us with his power, to change our world. You can make a difference. In God's hands, *you* can change the course of history.

113

13. Lions and Bicycles

"Be sober, be vigilant; because your adversary the devil walks about like a roaring lion, seeking whom he may devour." (1 Peter 5:8).

The Bible tells us that the devil walks about like a roaring lion, seeking whom he may devour. Yet in the face of this scripture, many Christians act passively towards the devil. They hope he won't trouble their life, but they don't take any steps to make sure he doesn't. The devil has no authority in the life of the believer except that which you give him. In the very beginning Adam was given authority and dominion over all creation. But he gave it away to Satan. When we receive Christ as our Saviour, our authority over Satan is restored. But he is a legalist and won't give up his power over parts of your life unless you claim them for Christ.

He is like a roaring lion seeking someone to devour. We cannot be passive in the presence of a roaring lion. Once, when I was in Africa, I was taken to Uganda's National Park to see the wildlife. Now, in Britain we have some wildlife parks, but they are all surrounded by a fence. I thought it would be the same in Uganda. But as we approached the National Park, we came over the brow of a hill and there before us, as far as the eye could see, stretched the vast African Savannah, with no fence!

As we drove along the road into the centre of the park we saw warthogs, hyenas, elephants and many other wild animals. What amazed me was that some people were cycling up to the hotel to deliver bananas. It struck me as being a little dangerous, cycling through this place when lions were walking about freely. The other thing I wondered was, how do the lions know where the boundaries of the National Park are?

On one trip to this place, a group of us were driving round in a minibus when the driver stopped the bus and said, "Look!

There are some lions. Everybody off the bus to see them." I thought to myself, "No. There are some lions. Everybody stay on the bus and let's keep moving!" Lions are dangerous. You can't be passive in their presence. I did get off the bus to look at the lions eventually, but only because they were a long way off.

On another occasion, we saw no lions. When we arrived back in Kampala, the capital city, I read an interesting story in the newspaper. We had seen no lions because they had walked into the nearest town and caused devastation. People had gone to bed and left a goat tied to the side of the house. When they got up in the morning there was just a bloodstained rope there. The goat had been devoured. The lions had been walking about, seeking whom they might devour. A night watchman was returning home on his bicycle at five o'clock in the morning when he was clawed off his bicycle by a roaring lion. He picked up his bicycle and hit the lion with it, as hard as he could. The lion ran away. He resisted the lion and it ran away. The Bible says, *"Therefore submit to God. Resist the devil and he will flee from you."* (James 4:7).

I once watched with horror, as the BBC news showed a mentally ill man who had climbed into the lion pit at a zoo. The lions came and killed him. He didn't resist them. He was mentally ill. He was passive in the presence of a roaring lion. He died a terrible death.

There is only one man I know who remained passive in the presence of hungry lions and yet was saved. His name was Daniel. He was put in the lions' den because he worshipped the living God. God performed a miracle and shut the mouths of the lions. In fact, Daniel seemed passive, but his faith was very active while he was in the lions' den. The purpose of this miracle was to prove the power of Almighty God. In fact, the king changed his beliefs and began to worship the one true God.

"Then King Darius wrote to all the peoples, nations and

116

men of every language throughout the land:

"May you prosper greatly!

I issue a decree that in every part of my kingdom people must fear and reverence the God of Daniel.

For he is the living God and he endures for ever; his kingdom will not be destroyed, his dominion will never end. He rescues and he saves; he performs signs and wonders in the heavens and on the earth.

He has rescued Daniel from the power of the lions." (Daniel 6:25-27 NIV).

Daniel had authority over the lions. God has given every believer authority over the devil when he walks about like a roaring lion. We must not sit passively by and watch the devil destroy our families, our health, our finances, our lives. We must resist him. When we do, he has to flee from us because God declared it in his word: *"Resist the devil and he will flee from you."* (James 4:7). We need to take our bicycle and deal the devil a blow on the head in the name of Jesus.

Another thing about lions is they are lazy. When they're hungry and see a herd of antelope, they never get the most athletic one at the front of the herd. In fact, they will never know what a juicy, healthy antelope tastes like. They always go the way of least resistance. They look for the one trailing behind the herd. The weakest one, trailing behind, probably full of self-pity. The one that is totally focussed on its own problems and hasn't really noticed how far behind it has got. The lion separates this one from the rest of the herd and then it pounces.

The devil works in the same way as the lion. He looks for the weakest one, the one full of self-pity, the one trailing behind. He will isolate this one and go for the jugular. Jesus said about the devil, *"The thief does not come except to steal, and to kill, and to destroy. I have come that they may have life, and that they may have it more abundantly."* (John 10:10).

117

The devil comes only to steal, kill and destroy. But Jesus has come to overthrow the works of the devil. *"The reason the Son of God appeared was to destroy the devil's work."* (1 John 3:8, NIV). Every born-again believer has authority over the devil. The devil has some power, and we should not underestimate him. But authority wins over power every time. A juggernaut has power. If you jumped in front of one, it would flatten you and you would die. But if a policeman, who has authority, steps into the path of an oncoming juggernaut and commands it to stop, it will, because he has authority to stop traffic. Jesus gives us his authority over the devil. *"Then He called His twelve disciples together and gave them power and authority over all demons, and to cure diseases."* (Luke 9:1). Another time he said to them, *"Behold, I give you the authority to trample on serpents and scorpions, and over all the power of the enemy, and nothing shall by any means hurt you."* (Luke 10:19).

Now we need to understand where the power is. The power is in Jesus. The most powerful weapon the devil has is death. That is his ultimate goal for everyone on the earth. Unfortunately for him, he tried his best weapon on Jesus. He managed to get him nailed to a cross, and watched as Jesus was buried in the grave. But death could not hold him and Jesus rose from the dead. Having conquered death itself, he proved that he has authority over the devil. The blood of Jesus paid the price for the sin of the whole world and dealt a fatal blow to the devil from which he will never recover. Like anyone who tends to overact, he is taking a long time to finish dying.

We are called to be overcomers and the Christian life is war. 1 John 2:14 says, *"I have written to you, young men, Because you are strong, and the word of God abides in you, And you have overcome the wicked one."* The way to overcome the devil is through the word of God, the Bible. When Jesus was tempted in the wilderness, he met every temptation with the word of

God. Every answer begins, *"It is written... It is written... It is written..."* (Matthew 4). When we face the roaring lion we need the whole armour of God. St Paul writes,

"Finally, my brethren, be strong in the Lord and in the power of His might. Put on the whole armour of God, that you may be able to stand against the wiles of the devil. For we do not wrestle against flesh and blood, but against principalities, against powers, against the rulers of the darkness of this age, against spiritual hosts of wickedness in the heavenly places. Therefore take up the whole armour of God, that you may be able to withstand in the evil day, and having done all, to stand.

Stand therefore, having girded your waist with truth, having put on the breastplate of righteousness, and having shod your feet with the preparation of the gospel of peace; above all, taking the shield of faith with which you will be able to quench all the fiery darts of the wicked one. And take the helmet of salvation, and the sword of the Spirit, which is the word of God;" (Ephesians 6:10-17).

Paul wrote these words from prison where he was surrounded by Roman soldiers. As he wrote to the church at Ephesus, he used the guard, who stood outside the door, as a visual aid. Rome's strength was in its organised army and the strategies it used. Paul teaches us that we can be even more powerful in warfare than the Roman army, which had conquered so much of the known world. But we need all our armour.

The first part of our spiritual armour is the belt of truth. The belt will hold all the other body armour together. We have to walk in truth. We have to be full of the truth, the word of God. We must love the scriptures, read, learn, mark and inwardly digest them. We must have him who said, *"I am the Truth"*, living inside us.

Second is the breastplate of righteousness. This breastplate is not of our righteousness but Christ's, which he freely gives those who serve him.

"...those who receive abundance of grace and of the gift of righteousness will reign in life through the One, Jesus Christ." (Romans 5:17).

"...be found in Him, not having my own righteousness, which is from the law, but that which is through faith in Christ, the righteousness which is from God by faith." (Philippians 3:9).

Thirdly, we need the shoes of the gospel of peace. We need to be prepared to speak about our faith. The shoes symbolise the going of the gospel. Jesus' parting words were, *"Go into all the world and preach the gospel to all creation."* We may not be a preacher in the usual sense of the word, but we must have a heart for the lost and be ready to speak of Christ when opportunities arise. Ready to give a reason for the hope that is in us.

Next is the shield of faith. Roman shields were covered with leather and before battle commenced they were soaked in water. It was this that put out the arrows of fire when they met with the wet shield. The shield is our faith. Faith that we are saved through Christ. Faith that we have his authority over the devil. We need to be soaked, drenched, dunked, immersed and baptised in the Holy Spirit and the blood of Jesus Christ. Then we will extinguish all the fiery darts of our enemy.

Then, the helmet of salvation. We need to protect our mind, the knowledge that we are saved through Christ. His blood has paid the price. The devil may try to remind you of things in your past and suggest that you are not saved. When he reminds you of your past, remind him of his future.

"... the everlasting fire prepared for the devil and his angels." (Matthew 25:41).

The armour is not a pick and mix option. 'Armour' is singular. Put on the whole armour of God. Jesus Christ is the armour of God. We need to be clothed in him. When the devil prowls around your life like a roaring lion, remember that if you have received Jesus Christ into your heart, you have the power to overcome. You have Jesus, the Anointed One and his Anointing living in you. In Revelation 5, Jesus is called the *'Lion of the tribe of Judah'*. He has already overcome the devil and in his name, and in his power, we, too, will overcome all the schemes of the evil one. Today, stop being passive. Put on the armour of God - clothe yourself with Jesus Christ - and in his Name, resist the devil and he will flee from you.

14. How to Walk on Water.

"During the fourth watch of the night Jesus went out to them, walking on the lake. When the disciples saw him walking on the lake, they were terrified. "It's a ghost," they said, and cried out in fear. But Jesus immediately said to them: "Take courage! It is I. Don't be afraid."

"Lord, if it's you," Peter replied, "tell me to come to you on the water."

"Come," he said. Then Peter got down out of the boat, walked on the water and came towards Jesus." (Matthew 14:25-29).

The first principle of walking on water is, has Jesus called you? *"Lord, if it's you," Peter replied, "tell me to come to you on the water."*

"Come," he said.

God calls us all to do something. Ephesians 2:10 says, *"For we are God's workmanship, created in Christ Jesus to do good works, which God prepared in advance for us to do."* There is something specific that God is calling you to do. When we walk in our calling with God, incredible things happen. So many people in the world today take the so-called safe option. Many spend their lives preserving history and tradition. Others spend their lives studying history. God calls us to spend our lives making history. Hebrews 11 is a catalogue of history makers who lived by faith. Here are just a few examples:

"By faith Abel offered God a better sacrifice than Cain did.

By faith he was commended as a righteous man, when God spoke well of his offerings. And by faith he still speaks, even though he is dead.

By faith Enoch was taken from this life, so that he did not experience death; he could not be found, because God had taken him away. For before he was taken, he was commended as one who pleased God. And without faith it is impossible to please God, because anyone who comes to him must believe that he exists and that he rewards those who earnestly seek him.

By faith Noah, when warned about things not yet seen, in holy fear built an ark to save his family.

By faith Abraham, when called to go to a place he would later receive as his inheritance, obeyed and went, even though he did not know where he was going.

By faith Joseph, when his end was near, spoke about the exodus of the Israelites from Egypt and gave instructions about his bones.

By faith Moses' parents hid him for three months after he was born, because they saw he was no ordinary child, and they were not afraid of the king's edict.

By faith Moses, when he had grown up, refused to be known as the son of Pharaoh's daughter. He chose to be ill-treated along with the people of God rather than to enjoy the pleasures of sin for a short time. He regarded disgrace for the sake of Christ as of greater value than the treasures of Egypt, because he was looking ahead to his reward.

By faith the people passed through the Red Sea as on dry land; but when the Egyptians tried to do so, they were drowned.

By faith the walls of Jericho fell, after the people had marched around them for seven days.

By faith the prostitute Rahab, because she welcomed the spies, was not killed with those who were disobedient.

And what more shall I say? I do not have time to tell about Gideon, Barak, Samson, Jephthah, David, Samuel and the prophets, who through faith conquered kingdoms, administered justice, and gained what was promised; who shut the mouths of lions, quenched the fury of the flames, and escaped the edge of the sword; whose weakness was turned to strength; and who became powerful in battle and routed foreign armies. Women received back their dead, raised to life again."

When Jesus calls us to come to him and walk by faith, we can be sure of his provision.

The second principle is to keep your eyes on Jesus. *"But when he saw the wind, he was afraid and, beginning to sink, cried out, "Lord, save me!"*

Immediately Jesus reached out his hand and caught him. "You of little faith," he said, "why did you doubt?" (Matthew 14:30-31).

When we trust God who we cannot see, we must be careful not to focus on the storms of life that we can see. 2 Corinthians 5:7 says, *"For we walk by faith, not by sight."* Whenever we try to move in faith, Satan will try to scare us into taking our eyes off Jesus. If we do, we will sink like Peter did. But even then, he called out to Jesus and Jesus rescued him. What an amazing God! An old chorus says,

Turn your eyes upon Jesus.
Look full in his wonderful face.
And the things of earth will grow strangely dim,
In the light of his glory and grace.

Hebrews 12:2 says, *"looking unto Jesus, the author and finisher of our faith..."*

The golden rule of walking on water, and indeed of life, is to keep your eyes on Jesus.

The third principle is, that it is very different from walking on firm ground. Living and acting 'by faith' is very different from acting by reason. Most of the time Peter walked on the ground like everybody else. But at this point in his life, Jesus called him to walk on water. If we are going to be obedient to God, we must train ourselves to be spiritually amphibious.

A modern day example.

1998 was a turning point in my life. In that year God called me to live 'by faith'. Now, all believers live by faith. We believe that Jesus Christ has paid the price for our sin and that through him we are acceptable to God the Father and will one day be received into heaven as a precious, blessed child. The Bible says, *"that if you confess with your mouth the Lord Jesus and believe in your heart that God has raised Him from the dead, you will be saved."* (Romans 10:9). We cannot prove that. We believe it to be true and act as though it is true. That's faith. The Bible says, *"Now faith is being sure of what we hope for and certain of what we do not see."* (Hebrews 11:1).

What God now called me to do was to live by faith in the area of our finances. That we would trust him for all our income. That, in Christ, we would be *'sure of what we hope for and certain of what we do not see'*. I had tried desperately to avoid this for a long time. God knew I would go anywhere and do anything so long as I didn't have to 'live by faith' in this sense of the phrase.

At the time, I was coming to the end of my second contract with the diocese in Suffolk. For 9 years they had paid me a regular income and housed me in a large, detached house in a quiet cul-de-sac. Council tax and water rates, telephone bill and several other financial burdens had all been taken care of by the diocese and the parish. But now I received a letter telling me that from September that year my contract would end and we would be required to leave the house the Church had provided us with for all those years.

A few years earlier I had set up a Trust called The Evangelism Fellowship, that held finances for our overseas missions and our publishing ministry. I sounded out the trustees about the Trust becoming my employer. But as they pointed out, our total annual income for the previous year was only £5,000. If the Trust was to maintain its current level of ministry and, in addition, employ me and meet all the costs of ministry the diocese had been meeting, we needed a minimum of £30,000 annual income. That would just be to maintain the current level of ministry. But God was calling us to expand the ministry. It seemed impossible, but with God all things are possible.

One option would have been to move to another area and start all over again in another parish. But I knew in my heart that God was calling me to *'step out of the boat and walk on water'*.

Hazel and I talked about renting a place to live. God seemed to have other plans and told us to *'possess the land'*. We were to buy a house. We had no savings at all, so how could we even begin to think about buying a house.

During this period of decision, lots of people offered their opinions about what we should do. You know, the church is a wonderful group of people. If you want to know your shortcomings, you won't find more helpful people anywhere. Some said, 'Go for it!' Others said, 'Don't do it.' The hard thing was that a few people we really respected said, 'Don't do it.' I got so confused I knew I had to hear from God. I prayed that, if we were to take this huge step of faith, God would give us a clear sign that he would provide for us financially. I didn't tell him what that sign should be, but I asked that he would make it very obvious.

Just seven days later I was preaching in church about encouragement. After the service a couple asked to have a private word with me. We found a quiet corner of the church and they handed me an envelope.

"We want to give you this." they said.

"Shall I open it now?" I asked.

"Yes." they said.

I opened the envelope to find a cheque for £6,500 for the Trust.

"Now tell me," I said, after getting over the initial shock, "why have you given me this? Did you hear about my contract coming to an end?"

"No." they said. "We don't know anything about that. God told us to give it to your ministry."

They told me how it had initially been a struggle because the husband had only been a Christian for a few weeks. But both of them had prayed and God had laid me on their heart.

Call me naive, but I took this as a sign from God that he would provide for us. God bless those who listen to you when you tell them to bless others. The ministry finances increased from that day. But now we needed a similar miracle in our personal finances.

So now what was the next step? How do you buy a house with faith? One of the things I have learnt over the years is that part of putting faith into action is to begin to act as though God has already provided for your needs. *"Now faith is being sure of what we hope for and certain of what we do not see."* (Hebrews 11:1). So we began looking in estate agents' windows and viewing houses, as though we had the means to buy one. The details of a house were sent through and it seemed unsuitable. However, as we were going to view a house the next day, we arranged to view this seemingly unsuitable house as well, just to eliminate it. But when we went to view it, it turned out to belong to an old friend of ours with whom we had lost touch. He was eager to sell it as he was moving out in a week's time, relocating to London for his new job.

We all liked the house. Although it didn't meet all our criteria, it sort of felt right. We made the owner an offer and he accepted it but on the condition that we started the purchase process immediately. I protested that the next day I was leaving for a three week mission to Africa. But he insisted that we had to get things moving the next day or the deal was off, because he needed a quick sale. I said I would see what I could do. But I didn't hold out much hope.

The next day was Friday and I had to leave for the airport by twelve noon. I had been looking into mortgages and went to a bank that seemed to have the best deal. All four mortgage advisors were unable to see me. I was offered an appointment but this was no good as I was leaving for Africa by noon. I went to my bank but the deals they offered had so many extra charges that I decided this was not of God.

I stepped out of the bank into the market square. It was 11 o'clock. One hour to go. Under my breath, I said to God, "You know I am out of my depth. I have tried everything I know how to do and I have failed. I am now going to walk across the road and tell the estate agent that I have failed to meet the vendor's conditions and to leave the house on the market. If you want us to have this house God, then you are going to have to do something."

I went into the estate agents' and told him I had totally failed in my quest to get a mortgage application started.

"Don't give up yet." he said, getting up from his desk. "Let me take you to meet someone who can help you."

The yellow danger light came on in my mind.

"His advice won't cost you anything and he's not connected with our company." he assured me.

The danger light changed from yellow to red. We walked up the road to another office. "Just see Adrian and then you will also need to get a solicitor."

The danger light was now flashing red and producing a little smoke.

I was taken into an office and sat thinking. What's happening? Twenty minutes to go before I leave for Africa and I'm right out of my depth. The door opened and in walked Adrian.

"Now what's the rush? Why did you have to see me straight away? he asked.

"I'm leaving for Africa in twenty minutes." I said.

"Really? What are you going to do there?"

Here we go again, I thought. "I'm going on a Christian mission to preach and teach the Bible." I said.

"Oh. I worship in Ipswich and our church has a project in Africa." he said.

The danger light suddenly stopped flashing and smouldering, and went off!

Adrian was so helpful and assured me that he didn't foresee any problems. There would be some papers to sign on my return from Africa. All I had to do now, with less than ten minutes to go, was to find a solicitor. Surely I would still be thwarted. Just at that moment, a man came into Adrian's office and announced he was a solicitor who had just opened a business across the road. He gave Adrian a price list for house conveyancing, and said to send to him anyone looking for a solicitor. Moments later I was in his office exchanging details. At two minutes to twelve I was back in the estate agents' with all the details he needed.

"Congratulations!" he beamed. "It's been quite a day for you. Got a mortgage, found a solicitor, bought a house, and now you're off to Africa. As you do!"

A few hours later, I sat with my friends Derek Ames and Adam Waller on a DC10. Power surged through the engines throwing the plane forward down the runway and into the air. "Oh dear!" I thought, "I've just bought a house!" The huge plane, weighing many tons, lifting into the air with no visible means of support, seemed very symbolic of what had just happened in my life. As I write this a year later, I can testify to God's amazing provision. He is a faithful God. We have never lacked the finances to pay the bills. We have had moments of fear, but that was because we stopped looking at Jesus and looked at the storm clouds. When you keep your eyes fixed on Jesus, you can walk on water.

15. Talking to Mountains

"For assuredly, I say to you, whoever says to this mountain, `Be removed and be cast into the sea,' and does not doubt in his heart, but believes that those things he says will be done, he will have whatever he says. Therefore I say to you, whatever things you ask when you pray, believe that you receive them, and you will have them." (Mark 11:23,24).

Jesus says that faith can move mountains. The mountains that block our path, the obstacles in our life. Sometimes we allow things to come against us and thwart our progress because they just seem overwhelming to us. But Jesus said we don't even need a large amount of faith to move mountains. *"...if you have faith as a mustard seed, you will say to this mountain, `Move from here to there,' and it will move; and nothing will be impossible for you."* (Matthew 17:20).

"Nothing will be impossible for you." It seems strange to speak to animate and inanimate objects and situations, and expect something to happen, but Jesus did it and taught his disciples to do the same. He told a fig tree to drop dead, and it did, (Mark 11:14,20). He told skin with leprosy to be cleansed and it was (Matt 8:3). He spoke to demons and sickness and drove them out (Matt 8:16). He spoke to a storm and it became calm (Matt 8:26). He told a crippled man to stand up, and he did. (Matt 9:6). He told a man who couldn't stretch his hand out to stretch his hand out, and he was able to. (Matt 12:13). He told Peter that he would find money to pay their tax bill, in the mouth of the first fish he caught and it was so. (Matt 17:27).

After the day of Pentecost, we see the disciples doing the same things as Jesus - speaking to mountains and commanding them to be removed. Peter said to a lame man, "Rise up and walk." And the man did. (Acts 3:6). He told Sapphira that she would be buried with her husband for lying to the Holy Spirit, and she dropped dead right there in front of him. (Acts 5:9). Paul spoke to a man who was crippled from birth saying, "Stand up straight on your feet!" And he leaped and walked." (Acts 14:10).

Both Jesus and the disciples proved the Scripture which says, *"Death and life are in the power of the tongue, And those who love it will eat its fruit."* (Proverbs 18:21). Believing something in our heart, and speaking it with our mouth, can bring things into being, because of the law of faith. Of course, that is how we become a believer. Paul says, *"that if you confess with your mouth the Lord Jesus and believe in your heart that God has raised Him from the dead, you will be saved."* (Romans 10:9). Yet for many Christians, that's the last time they use this faith principle. But it applies to every situation in our life. And it can be negative as well as positive. I cringe when I hear people saying they are *'sick to death of...'* Or they say, *'It makes me sick...'* If you keep saying it and believing it, you may speak it into being.

We are made in God's image. When he created the world, he did it through words and faith. He said, *'Let there be Light.'* And there was. The whole work of creation was accomplished by speaking things into being through faith. If we wake up every day and say, *'Everything is going to go wrong today',* and we believe it in our heart, we are in danger of bringing that thing into being. Much better to feed on God's word and what he says about us, and believe that and speak that out, and be in danger of good things happening to us. In the Anglican communion service, the congregation are told to *"feed on Him in your hearts, by faith, with thanksgiving."*

We have to find what God says in his word about our situation, believe it in our heart and speak it with our mouth - feed on it in our hearts, by faith, with thanksgiving. The revivalist, Smith Wiggleworth, used to say, *"God said it. I believe it. That settles the matter."* Unfortunately, many of us don't believe it. We look at what the Bible says, but we find it hard to believe it applies to us. That's because we are bombarded with doubt and cynicism every day. Cynicism is the cancer of British life. For decades we have heard the devil's doubts and the fears he whispers into our ears. We have meditated so long on our disappointments, we find it difficult to believe anything more than that God may one day allow us into heaven.

The basis of faith is very simple. So simple a child could understand it. - *God good - devil bad.* Jesus put it this way, *"The thief does not come except to steal, and to kill, and to destroy. I have come that they may have life, and that they may have it more abundantly."* (John 10:10). The book of Job is the classic account of tragedy. But it is Satan who came to steal and to kill and destroy. Job said *"Naked I came from my mother's womb, And naked shall I return there. The LORD gave, and the LORD has taken away; Blessed be the name of the LORD."* (Job 1:21). But it wasn't the Lord who took away, it was Satan. (Job 2:7). God had been the one who had made Job wealthy in the first place. (Deuteronomy 8:18). And God was the one who restored him after Satan had finished attacking him. (Job 42:12 - 17).

So God promises good things for his children. *"No eye has seen, no ear has heard, no mind has conceived what God has prepared for those who love him"* (1 Corinthians 2:9, NIV). All the promises that God has made in his word apply to all his children, to those who are in Christ. *"For all the promises of God in Him are Yes, and in Him Amen, to the glory of God through us."* (2 Corinthians 1:20). So we need to find the promise for our situation and begin speaking to our mountain. For example, if we are sick we could begin speaking over our body *"He Himself took [my] infirmities And bore [my] sicknesses."* (Matthew 8:17). Jesus bore our sickness, so we don't have to.

If we are in need financially, we could claim God's promise in 2 Corinthians 9:8, *"And God is able to make all grace abound toward [me], that [I], always having all sufficiency in all things, may have an abundance for every good work."*

If we are in trouble we could claim another promise, *"No weapon formed against [me] shall prosper, and every tongue which rises against [me] in judgment [I] shall condemn. This is the heritage of the servants of the LORD, And [my] righteousness is from the LORD."* (Isaiah 54:17).

Now it may be that we have to recite and memorise these Scriptures for a while before we begin to believe them. We may have to oil the wheels of our faith by speaking out the word even when we don't really believe it yet, because faith comes by hearing (Rom 10:17). As we dig into the word of God, faith will rise up in us. It may start as small as a mustard seed, but if we water it with the word of God it will grow.

"And [Jesus] said, "The kingdom of God is as if a man should scatter seed on the ground, and should sleep by night and rise by day, and the seed should sprout and grow, he himself does not know how. For the earth yields crops by itself: first the blade, then the head, after that the full grain in the head. But when the grain ripens, immediately he puts in the sickle, because the harvest has come... To what shall we liken the kingdom of God? Or with what parable shall we picture it? It is like a mustard seed which, when it is sown on the ground, is smaller than all the seeds on earth; but when it is sown, it grows up and becomes greater than all herbs, and shoots out large branches, so that the birds of the air may nest under its shade." (Mark 4:26-32).

When our faith begins to grow we will receive a harvest of what we prayed for - the removal of a mountain of sickness, lack or trouble. If we can come into agreement with others about the promise of God for our situation, we will have added power to our prayer.

"Again I say to you that if two of you agree on earth concerning anything that they ask, it will be done for them by My Father in heaven." (Matthew 18:19).

For married people, the obvious partner for the prayer of agreement is your spouse. But it is also good for men to find another man to come into agreement with, and for women another woman. David and Jonathan came into agreement for David's protection, when Saul, Jonathan's father, was trying to kill David (1 Samuel 20). They went further than being in agreement, they made a covenant. Nevertheless, they did stand in agreement for David's safety and it was granted.

God is the King of all things. When we are born again as his child, we enter into that royal family. We become princes or princesses in the kingdom of God. We come into the blood covenant with God and have certain blood bought rights and authority in the earth. This is not arrogance, it is what God wanted for his children.

"You ...have redeemed us to God by Your blood... And have made us kings and priests to our God; And we shall reign on the earth." (Revelation 5:9,10).

Jesus gave his disciples authority and power to move in the earth (Luke 10:19). Our purpose on earth, until Jesus returns, is to enforce the victory that Jesus won over Satan. Jesus said we should pray, *"Your kingdom come. Your will be done on earth as it is in heaven."* (Matthew 6:10). The politicians of our day do not have the answers to the problems in the nations. It is time for the children of God to rise up and declare peace and healing and blessing on the nations.

For many years now, I have visited our African partners in Uganda. Uganda is an interesting country. During the brutal reign of Idi Amin, murders were carried out by soldiers for fun. A baby was once tossed in the air and caught on a soldier's bayonet. This level of brutality was very common. Christians were a special target as Amin tried to make the nation an Islamic State. Rivers of blood ran in the street. An old Ugandan Christian told me of how he was imprisoned awaiting execution. Miraculously he escaped. But as he was fleeing the prison along a dark corridor, he thought there must have been a burst water pipe as he was ankle deep in what he thought was water. As he came into the light and looked down, he saw to his horror that it wasn't water, but a river of blood flowing from Amin's death chambers.

Other friends tell of secret prayer meetings in mosquito infested swamps where soldiers wouldn't come. The penalty for being caught praying was instant death. It was there, the Christians tell me, that Amin was overthrown. The victory over this dark mountain of bloodshed, was won in the swamp prayer meetings. Both Amin and his brutal successor were overthrown by the mountain-moving faith of ordinary Christians.

For over a decade, they have had relative stability and peace in most of Uganda. The President's wife and children are all practising Christians. The President, Yoweri Museveni, claims not to be a Christian, but seems very influenced by the teachings of Jesus. And for the population, he seems to be an answer to prayer. It is said that, during Museveni's visit to Libya, Col. Gaddaffi offered him a copy of the Koran. Museveni returned the gift saying that someone had once given him a Bible and he hadn't finished putting that into practice yet. The following speech is said to have been given by President Museveni at a regional meeting of African presidents held in Kampala.

"Thank you, Your Excellencies, for the opportunity to share some thoughts about the spiritual condition of the peoples of Africa. As I observe the tribal differences, religious divisions, poverty and disease, lack of sufficient educational opportunities for our children, political up-

heaval and racial strife, it becomes obvious that the principles of Jesus Christ have not penetrated Africa enough!

It may seem strange for some of you to think that I would say this about Christ, because I know many of you may think this is too religious and not a very practical solution to the problems I have just mentioned. Furthermore, I know that most of you do not think of me as a very religious man. In fact, I do not think that about myself. My wife is a much better believer and pray-er than I am, and those who have known me through the years know that I have had problems with religious people. As I have grown older, I realise that all of the problems have not been theirs, but I do think that those of us who claim to love God ought to love one another -- this is one of the most basic attributes of a follower of Christ.

As the years have gone by, however, even though I have not become a member of any special religious group, I have decided to follow Jesus Christ with my whole heart. I find in Him the inner strength, the precepts and the lifestyle that can help me and all the people of Uganda to solve the problems we face individually and as a nation.

It is one of the interesting facts about Jesus Christ that people in every nation of the world regardless of religion, whether one is a believer or a nonbeliever, consider Jesus the greatest authority on human relations in history. His views on that subject have transcended all religions and cultures. It is remarkable that the person of Jesus Christ is accepted by everyone - even when they are not attracted by institutional religion. With that in mind, I want to stress at least three significant precepts that Christ taught and modelled, which if practised, will help Africa: forgiveness, humility and love.

Forgiveness - Jesus Christ is the only Person ever to

come up with the idea of unconditional forgiveness, even of one's enemies. He went so far as to say, if you don't forgive, God won't forgive you. In countries where animosity and division go back for generations and even thousands of years, how can peace come to a person, a group of persons or a nation if at some point we do not forgive and let God take the vengeance on our enemies - if that is what He decides to do? It has also been discovered that if we do not forgive, in the final analysis, it hurts us more to hate than it does those we hate. Therefore, I have come to the conclusion that the message of Christ on forgiveness is the only practical solution to healing a nation's wounds and bringing unity.

Humility - this is one of the most important attributes necessary to become a good leader. When you observe leaders at all levels of society, throughout Africa and I suppose throughout the world, you find them being overcome by power, greed and self-interest. Somehow, after they have attained the prominence and positions of trust, they forget the people, their poverty and need. They forget that they could become a great instrument to help their country, and instead they begin to live like little kings and dictators.

Only with a humble spirit, one which recognises that we who have been given opportunities greater than most are in fact servants of God and the people rather than masters, will we be able to help our countries move from Third World status and lead the people to a new day. As the Scripture says, God resists the proud and gives help to the humble. If you have time to pray for me, please pray that God will give me the strength, wisdom and sense to be a humble servant.

Love - it has been fascinating to me to discover that

for centuries people who have been the most thoughtful, the most respected, and who have made the most lasting contributions to the human race have all agreed that the highest and greatest purpose for their lives has been to seek to love God with all their heart, mind, soul and strength. These are people like Moses - the great law-giver; Abraham - the man of faith and father of nations; William Wilberforce - the leader against the slave trade; Mother Teresa, and on and on. Jesus Christ said the sum of all the law and prophets is to love God and love one another.

If love for God and one another were the rule and the prevailing attitude in our nations and communities, all problems would move gradually to resolution. Even when love is not the rule for most of the population and only exists among the few, great things happen that give hope and life in a world starved of love and caring.

Today, as we meet together, let's resolve to take Jesus Christ out of the religious setting in which we have im-prisoned Him and walk with Him along the dusty roads of Africa where He feels much more at home."

If a group of poor African Christians can come together in agreement for a sea change in their nation with such staggering results as those in Uganda, then surely we can change the climate of our life, our family, our neighbourhood, and our nation.

Whatever mountain stands in your way today, it can be removed by faith, by prayer and by believing God's word. *"For the mountains shall depart And the hills be removed, But My kindness shall not depart from you, Nor shall My covenant of peace be removed," Says the LORD, who has mercy on you."* (Isaiah 54:10).

16. Remember Mrs Lot...

Jesus warned the disciples about being like Mrs Lot. *"Remember Lot's wife."* (Luke 17:32). God told Lot and his family not to look back when they left Sodom and Gomorrah, just prior to its destruction. But Lot's wife didn't follow God's word. She looked back. As she did, she died. Too many people today are wasting their time looking back. Don't be one of them. As followers of Jesus, we must refuse the past its desire to dominate our future. As I look around me, I see too many people turning into hamsters. They go round and round the wheel of yesterday and they never get anywhere.

Most of us bear the scars of past hurts. We can't change the past. We cannot unscramble eggs. But sometimes we spend too long sifting over the past. If we are not careful we will become like Mrs Lot - dry, bitter and useless to God. Jesus said, *"No one, having put his hand to the plough, and looking back, is fit for the kingdom of God."* (Luke 9:62). When a ploughman ploughs he has to keep his eyes forward and look where he is going. If he keeps looking back he'll be all over the place. If we are to become overcomers, we cannot allow the past to control us. The more we look back, the less able we are to see forward. Fear and regret work in much the same way as faith. The more we meditate on them, the more power they have in our life. I want you to know that the past makes no difference to what God can do in your life today. The Bible says, *"If anyone is in Christ, he is a new creation; old things have passed away; behold, all things have become new."* (2 Corinthians 5:17). God is powerful to do new things in, and with, your life. Your flesh will always want a pity-party every time someone says a harsh word, even if they are right. But we cannot let the flesh rule our life. We must restrain the flesh and retrain our soul. We must walk in the Spirit. St Paul wrote, *"One thing I do, forgetting those things which are behind and reaching forward to those things which are ahead, I press toward the goal for the prize of the upward call of God in Christ Jesus. "* (Philippians 3:13-14). Now Paul had every reason to turn over the past in his mind. His life had been incredible and he suffered much for the sake of the Kingdom. He wrote *"As servants of God we commend ourselves in every way: in great endurance; in troubles, hardships and distresses; in beatings, imprisonments and riots; in hard work, sleepless nights and hunger; in purity, understanding, patience and kindness; in the Holy Spirit and in sincere love; in truthful speech and in the power of God; with weapons of righteousness in the right hand and in the left; through glory and dishonour, bad report and good report; genuine, yet regarded as impostors; known, yet regarded as unknown; dying, and yet we live on; beaten, and yet not killed; sorrowful, yet always rejoicing; poor, yet making many rich; having nothing, and yet possessing everything. "* (2 Corinthians 6:3-10, NIV). He lived through a time of great persecution and suffering in the church, yet he did not skulk away and lick his wounds. He kept on *"forgetting those things which are behind and reaching forward to those things which are ahead",* in order to take hold of that for which Christ had taken hold of him.

The names of Jesus point to his desire to use broken vessels to show his glory in the earth. Redeemer. Saviour. Restorer of my soul. Lifter of my head. The Good Shepherd. In fact, the Bible teaches that God chooses the weaker things in the world. *"But God has chosen the foolish things of the world to put to shame the wise, and God has chosen the weak things of the world to put to shame the things which are mighty; and the base things of the world and the things which are despised God has chosen, and the things which are not, to bring to nothing the things that are, that no flesh should glory in His presence. "* (1 Corinthians 1:27-29).

It is the very wounds of Jesus that are most powerful. By his

144

wounds, I am healed. In his death is my life. It is time for you to rise up and stride boldly away from yesterday and step into your destiny as a child of the living God. It is time to focus on what God says about you, not what the world or circumstances say about you. It is time for the weak to say, *'I am strong.'* (Joel 3:10). It is time for the poor to say, 'I am rich', for the blind to say, 'I can see'.

We are called to be overcomers, people who make a difference in the world. We are called to be like Jesus, and grow more like him day by day. Jesus says to the church, *"To him who overcomes I will grant to sit with Me on My throne, as I also overcame and sat down with My Father on His throne."* (Revelation 3:21).

The way we overcome the world is through faith in God's word. Trusting what God has said more than what our circumstances tell us. This is the destiny of every born again believer. *"For everyone born of God overcomes the world. This is the victory that has overcome the world, even our faith."* (1 John 5:4, NIV). The principles I have outlined in this book are not a series of magic words. It is unlikely that we will declare God's word over our life one day, and always see dramatic results the next day. But the declaration of God's word, and putting our trust in God's word more than in our circumstances, has to become a lifestyle. **It has to become a lifestyle.** Like all of God's creation, faith grows and takes root. Jesus said, *"The kingdom of God is as if a man should scatter seed on the ground, and should sleep by night and rise by day, and the seed should sprout and grow, he himself does not know how. For the earth yields crops by itself: first the blade, then the head, after that the full grain in the head. But when the grain ripens, immediately he puts in the sickle, because the harvest has come."* Then He said, *"To what shall we liken the kingdom of God? Or with what parable shall we picture it? It is like a mustard seed which,* *when it is sown on the ground, is smaller than all the seeds on earth; but when it is sown, it grows up and becomes greater than all herbs, and shoots out large branches, so that the birds of the air may nest under its shade."* (Mark 4:26-32). So, declaring God's word over our life seems like a small 'mustard seed' thing to do. But if we make it a lifestyle and commit to it, we will eventually get the breakthrough.

Quite often, when I come to enforce the victory of Jesus in a new area of my life, as I declare what God has said and try to build faith in his word, things begin to get worse. Satan has held on to so much of our lives for so long, that he is not going to let go without a fight. In the area of healing or finances, things may get worse temporarily, before the breakthrough comes. But we must not let Satan intimidate us.

"When you go out to battle against your enemies, and see horses and chariots and people more numerous than you, do not be afraid of them; for the LORD your God is with you, who brought you up from the land of Egypt. So it shall be, when you are on the verge of battle, that the priest shall approach and speak to the people. And he shall say to them, 'Hear, O Israel: Today you are on the verge of battle with your enemies. Do not let your heart faint, do not be afraid, and do not tremble or be terrified because of them; for the LORD your God is He who goes with you, to fight for you against your enemies, to save you." (Deuteronomy 20:1-4). Jesus is the same yesterday, today and forever (Hebrews 13:8). This instruction that he gave to the Israelites about doing battle with their physical enemies, is the same instruction he gives to us as we fight our spiritual enemy, the devil. Satan is a master of intimidation. But we have to remember what God has already delivered us from. It is he who will do the fighting as we declare his word. God said to Jeremiah, *"I am ready to perform my word."* (Jeremiah 1:12). It is our job to speak out the word of God in prayer over our

situation. It is God's job, and delight, to perform his word. We have to speak out the word of God over the situation. It is no good just reading it and keeping it in your heart, you have to speak it out. In the temptation, Jesus overcame every attack of Satan with the word. *"It is written... It is written... It is written..."* He says three times. Then we read, *"Satan left him"*. Resist the devil and he will flee from you. Proverbs 18:21 says, *"The tongue has the power of life and death, and those who love it will eat its fruit."* We overcome by establishing God's truth in the situation. *"By the mouth of two or three witnesses every word shall be established."* (2 Corinthians 13:1). Jesus established his identity in this way in John 8:17. It was also the rule in criminal trials in Israel (Deuteronomy 19:15). Now take healing for example. Satan says we are sick and in decline.

God says we are healed. (Isaiah 53:5, Matthew 8:17). But both those claims only have one witness each. For either to be established, it requires a second witness. If we believe in our heart and confess with our mouth that we are sick and getting sicker every day, Satan's word will be established in our life. But if we come into agreement with God's word - believe it in our heart and confess it with our mouth - then we will establish God's word in our body, and in our life because we become the second witness. This is why it is so important to speak the answer and not the problem.

Study the story of David and Goliath in 1 Samuel 17 again and see how the Israelites were focusing on the problem and speaking the problem, but David came and focussed on the answer. And he spoke the answer, not the problem. He says in verse 26, *"Who is this uncircumcised Philistine that he should defy the armies of the living God?"* The key words are, "Uncircumcised" and "living God." Herein lay the answer. Israel was a covenant people, and the mark of circumcision was the reminder of the covenant. All that God had, was theirs. They were not just a bunch of Captain Mainwaring's home-guard odds and ends from Walmington-On-Sea. They were the army of the Living God - a chosen race, a holy people. David believed the word, spoke the word, and by the Spirit of the Living God, he enforced the word. And took away the shame from Israel. No wonder God chose him as king.

We have to become overcomers. Warriors of the word, enforcing the victory.

"For though we walk in the flesh, we do not war according to the flesh. For the weapons of our warfare are not carnal but mighty in God for pulling down strongholds, casting down arguments and every high thing that exalts itself against the knowledge of God, bringing every thought into captivity to the obedience of Christ." (2 Corinthians 10:3-5).

Today you must overcome your feelings. Feelings are a roller-coaster where the main event is downward. If you listen to your feelings and dwell on the past, you will always be dragged down. Today you have a decision to make. Will you let the past possess and control you? Or will you stride away from your past and step into your destiny, taking control over the present and the future, by faith in the word of God? The past is past. You cannot change it. The future is in your hands and in your mouth.

17. The White Stone

The matter of our identity is crucial. If we don't discover who we are, it will cause untold damage to ourselves and those around us. I have watched several people reach a mid-life crisis, and become so restless they were dangerous. Several of them ended up committing adultery and destroying their marriage. One man in particular, was a keen Christian and in a position of leadership in his church. He ran off with a woman almost half his age. He said that God understood him and was with him in his decision. That is utter rubbish, and more evidence of a loss of identity. It was said of him, that he had not had a wayward youth, but remained a faithful Christian during his teenage years. And those two ages - adolescence and mid-life - seem to be the two danger spots when our identity crisis can boil over and ruin our life.

The restlessness that an identity crisis causes, is not dissimilar to an unruly child thrashing about trying to find the boundaries for his behaviour. Friends of mine who have adopted children, all speak of a difficult settling in period when the adopted child becomes unruly because they are trying to find the limits of what is acceptable. They are trying to discover who they are in this new family. If we are to be used by God and find real peace with ourselves and with God, we must answer two questions: Who am I? And who is God?

If we read the Bible, we will see that this question about our identity is crucial to life on earth. In the very beginning, Satan attacked Adam and Eve at the point of their identity. *"Then the serpent said to the woman, "You will not surely die. For God knows that in the day you eat of it your eyes will be opened, and you will be like God, knowing good and evil."* (Genesis 3:4-5). He said to Eve, *'You will be like God...'* But she already was, she was made in his image, just as Adam was. Satan brought confusion about their identity. And the result was rebellion against God. A disaster. We can see the importance of identity right throughout the Bible.

When God decided to make a covenant with Abraham, the first thing he did was tell him to leave his father's house.

"Now the LORD had said to Abram: "Get out of your country, From your family And from your father's house, To a land that I will show you. I will make you a great nation; I will bless you And make your name great; And you shall be a blessing. I will bless those who bless you, And I will curse him who curses you; And in you all the families of the earth shall be blessed." (Genesis 12:1-3).

Now why did God tell him to leave his family? Well, we discover that Terah, Abraham's father, had worshipped demonic gods. *"Thus says the LORD God of Israel: 'Your fathers, including Terah, the father of Abraham ... dwelt on the other side of the River in old times; and they served other gods.'"* (Joshua 24:2). God had to enable Abraham to find his identity in God, not in Terah his natural father. Many Christians have limited themselves because they find their identity in their family, in their parents. They allow themselves to be limited by what their parents achieved or failed to achieve. But when we are born again into God's family, our identity becomes rooted in him, who is without limitations. We were created in God's image in the first place. If we try to take our identity from our fallen parents, however good they are or were, we will be limiting ourselves, and fail to reach our full potential in Christ. So Abraham settled the identity issue before being blessed by God and beginning a new nation.

When Moses was called by God to lead the Israelites out of Egypt, he first had to settle the identity issue. If ever a man was likely to have an identity crisis, Moses was. Born an Israelite, but brought up in Pharaoh's palace as an Egyptian. Having murdered an Egyptian who was beating an Israelite, he fled and became a fugitive in Midian. From a prince to a shepherd - the story of David in reverse. So when God called Moses to lead the people out of slavery, he had some questions.

"But Moses said to God, "Who am I that I should go to Pharaoh, and that I should bring the children of Israel out of Egypt?" (Exodus 3:11).

"Then Moses said to God, "Indeed, when I come to the children of Israel and say to them, 'The God of your fathers has sent me to you,' and they say to me, 'What is His name?' what shall I say to them?" (Exodus 3:13).

Basically, Moses said, "Who am I and Who are you?" When he was knocking on Pharaoh's door, it would not be the time to start asking, "Who am I to be doing this?" Self doubt at that point would have rendered Moses incapable of challenging Pharaoh. So Moses dealt with the identity issue right at the beginning.

Isaiah had a vision of God when king Uzziah died. *"In the year that King Uzziah died, I saw the Lord sitting on a throne, high and lifted up, and the train of His robe filled the temple... So I said: "Woe is me, for I am undone! Because I am a man of unclean lips, And I dwell in the midst of a people of unclean lips." ...Then one of the seraphim flew to me, having in his hand a live coal which he had taken with the tongs from the altar. And he touched my mouth with it, and said: "Behold, this has touched your lips; Your iniquity is taken away, And your sin purged." Also I heard the voice of the Lord, saying: "Whom shall I send, And who will go for Us?" Then I said, "Here am I! Send me." And He said, "Go, and tell this people..."* (Isaiah 6:1-9).

It was a time of national upheaval. The king had died. Isaiah saw a vision of the Lord, and suddenly his own identity was clear to him, *'I am a man of unclean lips...'* But God was looking for someone to speak the word of God. So the seraphim touched Isaiah's mouth and changed his identity. So when God said, *'Who shall I send?'* Isaiah said confidently, *"Here am I! Send me."* And God said, *"Go, and tell this people..."* Notice that God did not say, "No. We can't have a man with unclean lips, going to speak the word of God." No. He said, *"Go, and tell this people..."* In a moment, Isaiah had his marred identity exposed and changed - cleansed and ready to reach his full potential for God, when he started to see himself as God saw him.

Jeremiah had a poor self image, which caused an identity crisis when God called him. *"Then said I: "Ah, Lord GOD! Behold, I cannot speak, for I am a youth." But the LORD said to me: "Do not say, 'I am a youth,' For you shall go to all to whom I send you, And whatever I command you, you shall speak."* (Jeremiah 1:6-7). Jeremiah presumed that his age excluded him from serving God. But God said he had appointed him before he was born. So Jeremiah had to stop thinking of himself as *'...only a youth'* and start thinking of himself as a prophet to the nations.

Before Jesus went to the cross, he wanted to settle his own identity in the mind of the disciples. Jesus didn't have an identity problem, but faced with seeing him die on the cross, his disciples may have had misunderstandings about Jesus' identity.

"When Jesus came into the region of Caesarea Philippi, He asked His disciples, saying, "Who do men say that I, the Son of Man, am?" So they said, "Some say John the Baptist, some Elijah, and others Jeremiah or one of the prophets." He said to them, "But who do you say that I am?" Simon Peter answered and said, "You are the Christ, the Son of the living God." (Matthew 16:13-16). When Jesus said, *'On this rock I will build my church,'* he was not talking about Peter, but about the rock of the revelation of the identity of Jesus. Who Jesus is, is the rock

on which God builds everything. Jesus said the wise man is the one who builds his life on the rock of his word. Jesus is the rock of our life, the only sure foundation we can build on. The only foundation for knowing who we really are.

Whatever your identity has been in the past, in Jesus you have a new identity. *"Therefore, if anyone is in Christ, he is a new creation; old things have passed away; behold, all things have become new."* (2 Corinthians 5:17).

In Revelation 2:17 Jesus says, *"To him who overcomes... I will give him a white stone, and on the stone a new name written which no one knows except him who receives it."* Here, it seems, Jesus gives this rock of unshakable identity. The rock which has caused Christian martyrs to go joyfully to their death, because they knew who they were and who God was. The rock which has caused men and women of faith to do, and to endure, incredible things for the Kingdom of God.

When Jesus says he will give us a white stone, the Greek word translated *'white'* is *'leukos'* which means: *"light, bright, brilliant; brilliant from whiteness, (dazzling) white; of the garments of angels, and of those exalted to the splendour of the heavenly state; shining or white garments worn on festive or state occasions; of white garments as the sign of innocence and purity of the soul."*

The Greek word used for *'stone'* is *'psephos'* which carries the meanings of: *"a small worn smooth stone, a pebble; in the ancient courts of justice the accused were condemned by black pebbles and the acquitted by white; a vote (on account of the use of pebbles in voting)."*

He gives the white stone to those who overcome (Revelation 2:17). As we rise up and begin to believe what God says, as we refuse to be intimidated by the circumstances the devil throws at us; as we stand on God's promises and let God be true and every man a liar (Romans 3:4); so we will discover who we really are. As we exercise our faith in the affairs of our lives and those of our nation, so we will take hold of the white stone in the hand of Jesus.

For so long, too many Christians have held a shallow faith which has amounted to little more than a ticket to heaven. Today, God is calling you to become an overcomer, to fully understand faith in Jesus.

Philemon 6 says, "[And I pray] that the participation in *and* sharing of your faith may produce *and* promote full recognition *and* appreciation *and* understanding *and* precise knowledge of every good [thing] that is ours in [our identification with] Christ *Jesus - and* unto [His glory]. *(Amplified Bible)*.

The prayer is that in the sharing of our faith - that is, seeing and explaining how it works to others - we will produce a greater understanding and appreciation of all that is ours in Christ. Many Christians think God is trying to get them to heaven. But Jesus wants us to bring heaven down to earth. That is why he taught his disciples to pray, *"Your kingdom come. Your will be done On earth as it is in heaven." (Matthew 6:10).*

I pray that as you read and re-read the chapters of this book, your faith may grow and you will rise up and become an overcomer. That you would see the miracle-working, yoke-destroying, body-healing, anointing of God in your life. Today, when I look in the mirror, I no longer see a stranger looking back at me, but a child of the Living God, an overcomer, a prince in God's Kingdom, a joint heir with Christ, a man who was born in Manchester, but born again in the Kingdom of Heaven. Today, you do not need to see a stranger in the mirror. But as you receive Jesus as your personal Saviour, and put his word into practice, you can look into the eyes of an overcomer. You can look at one who has the Anointed One and his Anointing living and working in you. You can rise up and know who you are, and who he is. Arise!

The vision of Don Egan is to '*Go into all the world and preach the gospel to all creation.*' Not only the gospel of the cross and new life, but the full gospel of abundant life in Jesus Christ. Don is an evangelist and Bible teacher.

Don originally worked for Save the Children Fund in a deprived area of Manchester in Moss Side and Hulme. In 1987 he completed a three year diploma in evangelism studies with Church Army. He was admitted to the office of Evangelist by the Archbishop of Canterbury and was an assistant minister in several Anglican Churches from 1987 - 1998.

In 1994 he founded the Evangelism Fellowship, a charitable Trust, and became its Director. In 1998 he ceased being employed by the Diocese of St Edmundsbury & Ipswich and became the full time Director of the Evangelism Fellowship.

Don has ministered across the UK in many denominations and non-church settings. He has also ministered in The Philippines, Uganda, Rwanda, Tanzania, and Nigeria. He has preached to people from a wide variety of backgrounds. From refugees in Africa to finance executives at Lloyds of London. His Christian writings have reached tens of thousands of people in three languages.

In 1994, Don set up the Uganda Partnership which helps evangelists in Uganda meet basic and ministry needs.

In 1999, he set up the Prosper Project which gives small loans to people in Rwanda to set up in business.

The Evangelism Fellowship, which supports Don's ministry, relies on the partnership of people like you, to minister across the world.

If you would like to receive our free GO magazine, with news of this ministry and helpful articles by Don Egan and others, please fill in the slip opposite. GO magazine is sent free and without obligation.

You may photocopy this page if you don't want to cut the book!

Please send me your free "GO" magazine.

Name

Address

Postcode

Please write clearly in BLOCK CAPS.

Send this slip to:
The Evangelism Fellowship
P O Box 55
STOWMARKET
IP14 1UG

Tel: 01449 677058